YOU'RE
GONNA
MAKE IT

YOU'RE GONNA MAKE IT

JOHN BYTHEWAY

Deseret Book Company
Salt Lake City, Utah

Library of Congress Cataloging-in-Publication Data

Bytheway, John, 1962–
    You're gonna make it / by John Bytheway.
      p.   cm.
    Includes index.
    Summary: Offers advice and encouragement, based on testimony from the Gospel, on facing some of the common difficulties experienced by young people as they move from seventh grade on up through high school.
    ISBN 1-57345-301-3
    1. Teenagers—Religious life. 2. Teenagers—Conduct of life. 3. Church of Jesus Christ of Latter-day Saints—Doctrines—Juvenile literature. 4. Mormon Church—Doctrines—Juvenile literature. [1. Mormon Church—Doctrines. 2. Conduct of life. 3. Christian life.] I. Title.
BX8643.Y6B994   1997
248.8'3—dc21   97-18318
                                                    CIP
                                                         AC

Printed in the United States of America   72082-4585H

10   9   8   7   6   5   4   3   2

To my high-school friends in the Parley's Second Ward. Go P2!

Synde Larson Bell
Jonny Clark
Esther deLannoy Cloward
Jodie Czarnik Coon
Guy Duersch
Jim Morgan
Mike Morgan
Eric Myrberg
Scott Perry
John Romine
Steve Romine
Mike Schauerhamer
Steve Weldon
Susan Workman

Contents

Acknowledgments

You really know who your friends are when they agree to read something you hope might one day become a decent manuscript. For this I am indebted to Brad Wilcox, Kathy Schlendorf, Colleen Peterson, and Amy Loveridge. Their critical eye and helpful suggestions have made this a much better book than it would have been otherwise.

I am also grateful to Ron Millett, Sheri Dew, and all those at Deseret Book who are so good at what they do and who make the process so much fun. Special thanks to Emily Watts for her expert advice and editorial skills, and to Shauna Gibby for her graphic design work.

Mostly, I am thankful to my wife, Kimberly. Her constant encouragement, excitement, and energy have made life more wonderful than I ever imagined it could be.

Before We Begin,
Here's a Word from . . . a Word

Whoa, who turned on the lights? It was pretty dark in here until you opened the cover. Give me a second for my i's to adjust. . . .

Hi! We're a bunch of words. John will be using us to tell you all kinds of things. We've been sentenced to live in books. We may look like just a bunch of ink, but we're actually pretty powerful. Do you believe me? Think about it. I mean, who's in charge of your country right now? The President? Congress? Nope. It's words. It's a bunch of paragraphs called the Constitution. See what I mean? We're powerful. Wars have been started over words, and wars have been avoided with words. Words can make you sad, words can make you glad, and a few words from that special someone in math class can make you giddy. Words have had an impact on the whole world—and that's just a *participle* of what we can do!

There are old words, new words, long words, and short words. In fact, I went to a family reunion once. It was held in a dictionary. There were so many of us crammed in there, we couldn't get another word in edgewise. The UPPERCASES were there, the lowercases were there, and I had to brush up on my *italics.* Nothing but words as far as i could c, and I've never seen so many weird o's! Some of the older words just wanted to catch some z's, and it looked like a few of them slipped into a comma. We told the young'uns to mind their p's and q's, but they all wanted to play on the crosswords. One of them ran to the edge of the page and got hyphenated. We had a big word search at the end to get them all back. When I got home, I had sore footnotes. But boy oh boy, you should've seen the feast we had at the table of contents! Only problem was, it attracted a lot of b's.

But I'm getting off the subject. The dictionary was fun, except that there was no plot, no story, and no message! Words only make sense when they're in a certain *sequence* (you can only sit in alphabetical order for so long), so we need an author to get us in line. John Bytheway, our author, is going to arrange a bunch of us words for a specific reason. (*Bytheway:* now there's an interesting set of words. His last name is either one word or three words; it's hard to tell.) Anyway, he hopes to arrange words in such a careful sequence that they might even build your testimony and strengthen your faith! Words can do that, as I'm sure you've already learned from the words you've read in seminary. *Those* words, the words from the scriptures and the prophets, are the best you'll ever see. In fact, after the basic items people need for survival, the most important thing in their lives is words: "Man shall not live by bread alone, but by *every word* that proceedeth out of the mouth of God" (Matthew 4:4; emphasis added). See? I told you words were important!

Thanks for opening up this book and letting us see the light. It gets dark in here between the paperbacks. We wish more people like you would read books. This world would be a better place if more good words were seeing the light of day and more teenagers were being enlightened by words. Always remember, you can't judge a book by its cover, but you *can* judge a book by its words. Let's hope these words are good.

Well, it's time for the author to do the talking, so we're going to let John put us in order from now on. It's been nice chatting with you. Read us again soon! (We'll be in here, but we'll sound like your author—you can read us between the lines.)

HELLO DAY ASSEMBLY

The Standing Ovation I Didn't Like

Public Notice: The great and spacious building has been condemned to make room for the many mansions soon to be occupied by those who were not distracted by the pride and applause of the world.

What's going on here—is it you again? Don't you do anything besides read books? What kind of a teenager are you, anyway? Don't you ever watch TV or listen to the radio? "Be young!" they say. "Have fun!" they say. But no, you can't just be a normal teenager, can you? You insist on trying to improve your life and expand your mind by reading books. What is it with you? Are you trying to win a weirdo contest or something? *Teenagers don't read books,* don't you know? Teenagers just hang out at the mall, watch TV, play video games, and ask parents for money and rides.

Why do you insist on doing things people think you won't do? Why can't you just be average? I have an idea: Why don't you put this book down, and go buy a Slurpee? Quiet! . . . did you hear that? It's your stomach saying, "Buy me a Slurpee, buy me a Slurpee." Say, isn't it time for that fine, intellectual television program, *Saved by the Bell?* Hey, I hear a honk outside—your friends want to go drive around! Better put this book down and go do something fun. C'mon, reading is boring!

Hello? Are you still there? Well, I've tried everything I can to discourage you from reading this book, but it looks like you won't budge. Stubborn little camper, eh? Are you just bent on becoming incredible? Too late. You already are. I guess I'd better take it for granted that anybody reading this book is way beyond average. That means the pressure is really on me, 'cause I'm just an average guy, trying to talk to some of the world's finest teenagers!

What's that? You don't feel incredible? Well, I can understand that. When I was a teenager, I felt pretty average too. I didn't have a letterman's jacket because I didn't letter in anything. I was never prom royalty; I was never even asked to *escort* any of the prom royalty. I wasn't chosen as "most preferred" or "most likely to succeed" or the one with the "best smile." I didn't have a nice car. I wasn't a football hero or a basketball star. If you don't have any of those things, doesn't that mean you're average? Doesn't that mean you're just yearbook fodder? another face in the crowd? another student number in the computer?

No. It doesn't. I didn't fully comprehend it at the time, but I had something that billions of people on the earth didn't have. And so do you.

My main purpose in writing this book is to show you that you can make it through your toughest years in school if you will rely on the gospel. I *know* that is true because that's how I made it. I'm afraid that in order to accomplish this purpose, I'm going to have to use a lot of personal experiences about myself (mostly because I don't know any personal experiences about you). In fact, I'm hoping this book can count for all the journal entries I should have written when I was younger. Do you think that'll work? Yeah. Me neither.

But before I show you how the gospel can see you through, we have to make sure nothing else gets in the way. What could possibly get in the way of the gospel? The answer: almost anything. Anything that gets us off track or distracted. Anything that appears to be important when it really isn't. Anything that's widely accepted and applauded by the world, but is really empty and hollow.

For example, I've been seeing a new bumper sticker around lately that reads, "Trees are the answer." Think about that: "Trees are the answer." Oh, really? The first time I read that, I rolled my eyes so hard I almost rolled the car.

Trees are very nice, folks, but trees are *not* the answer. Jesus Christ is the answer. He created the trees. He created *us!* Can trees forgive us of our sins? Did trees suffer and die so that we could be clean? Did trees teach us the principles that would solve virtually every world problem (including the shrinking rain forests)? No. Jesus did.

An eighteenth-century British statesman, Edmund Burke, said: "The only thing necessary for evil to triumph over good is for good men to do nothing." Someone elaborated on that thought in our century: "Actually, the problem isn't that they're doing nothing. The problem is that they're doing something else." And that's the point. If Satan can't draw us into evil things, he'll just get us to focus on things that are nice, like trees, but that can distract us from the real answers.

Actually, it's easy to understand why people look to trees for answers. Trees are very quiet. Trees don't tell you how to live your life. Trees don't begin any sentences with "Thou shalt not . . . " Trees just sit there and look pretty and make oxygen. Now, there's an easy religion: "Folks, just do everything this tree tells you." Spare me.

Anyway, when I was in high school, I loved the gospel, but I didn't realize how much it could help me through the daily teenage routine. The distraction that got nearly everyone's undivided attention in high school was not trees, however. It was a list of concerns including popularity, image, dates, clothes, parties, and worrying over what everybody thought everybody else was doing. These things were a powerful distraction in my high school days; they still are today. Sometimes you might feel like you're about to be trampled in the mad stampede toward the great and spacious building. And if you're not careful, you might be.

Now, don't get me wrong, things like dates and clothes and parties have their place, but they need to be kept in their place. Just don't let them *re*-place the Lord and his gospel. If anything but the gospel comes first, no matter what it is, it's not worth it. William Law said it like this: "If you have not chosen the kingdom of God, it will make in the end no difference what you have chosen instead." (You might have to read that one a few times—my dad used to quote it all the time and I didn't get it.)

Most of the time, it's fairly easy to tell right from wrong. But this "distraction" business can be tricky. Often our distractions aren't bad, they're just not the best. In other words, sometimes good, noble, and worthwhile things distract us from the most important things. Even good things can be dangerous if they replace the best things. Want an example? Good. I'll give you one.

Some time after I returned home from my mission, the Lord blessed me with a great love for teenagers. I'm not sure why I enjoy them so much. Maybe it's because they're so hyper and curious and eager to learn. Maybe it's because I remember my own teenage years so well and am not quite ready to let them go. I don't know. All I know is that I love being with teens. I love talking to them, joking with them, and, most of all, I love sharing my feelings and faith with them.

I had a chance to do just that on a beautiful summer day a few years ago at BYU. Youth groups had descended on campus like a hungry swarm of crickets, and there wasn't a seagull in sight. I was in a great mood. I looked up at the summer sky, closed my eyes, and felt the warmth on my face as I quickened my pace to get to a speaking assignment in the Wilkinson Center Ballroom. About a thousand teenagers would be there. I can't remember if I was late or if I was substituting at the last minute for a speaker who had canceled, but I remember that the youth were already assembled as I began walking up the aisle in the back.

When they saw me coming in, a few of the young people stood on their feet and began to applaud. It soon spread to the other rows, until all the youth in the whole place were on their feet. At first I didn't know what was going on; I suspected that this little display of affection had been planned by some of the leaders and counselors. I was a little embarrassed, and all I could do was look at the floor and shake my head as I walked along. But as I lifted my eyes a little, and looked into a few of those young people's faces, I saw their sincerity, and I felt an overwhelming feeling of gratitude. "Aw, man," I thought to myself, "what a great group. What a great church. I love these guys!"

I am no longer a teenager, but I still have a lot of eighth-grader inside of me. For some reason, seeing all those happy, clapping, cheering youth as I walked up the aisle to the front (I felt like a new contestant on *The Price Is Right*) brought back a lot of junior high feelings. Back then I had often felt lost, misplaced, and out of the popular loop. Those somewhat painful memories, mixed with feelings of gratitude, swelled up inside of me until they pushed out a few tears on top. I was getting close to the podium now, and I had a problem—I didn't want to get all teary-eyed in front of teenagers. I don't like to further the false notion that "whoever cries the most is the most spiritual," so when I get too emotional I usually tell myself a joke or something. I looked at the floor and tried to lighten up, but it didn't work. I couldn't hide it anymore. Finally, I lifted my head, and I tried to explain my emotions to the young people. I told them about the sadness I'd felt in junior high school. I told them how often I had felt lost in the crowd, and how I had wondered if I would ever make it. Back in eighth grade, when I was dealing with all those feelings, I never could have imagined a group of my peers giving me such a generous welcome.

But something was wrong. Along with the joy I felt from their sincere applause, I had an awful pit in my stomach. First of all, I've never liked the idea of being famous, the object of adoring crowds. Let the publicity-hungry TV stars and the commercially hyped professional athletes have all that. I just wanted to be a teacher.

As the applause continued, the pit in my stomach grew into a rock because I was afraid those great young people were missing the point. I knew I shouldn't be the object of their affection. And maybe I wasn't; maybe they were just excited to be there. Maybe they were used to high school assemblies in which applause was encouraged or even desired. Maybe they were inspired by the great weather outside, or by the chance to be surrounded by so many other LDS youth.

But maybe it was worse. Maybe I was teaching the wrong way. Could I be getting in the way of the real message? Could I be a distraction from what really matters? I didn't know what to say or what to do. Then I had a flash of inspiration. I remembered a phrase I'd heard, something about a "spiritual eclipse." That was it. I would try to give the youth a brief lesson in what we might call "spiritual astronomy."

We all know what happens when the moon blocks out the sun; we call it an eclipse. And anything that eclipses the light of the sun causes darkness. Similarly, when anyone, anything, any hobby, any habit, any activity, or any person—even a well-meaning youth speaker—blocks out *the Son,* His gospel and His message, it causes a *spiritual eclipse.*

I didn't want to be an eclipse. I wanted to get completely out of the way and let the bright light of the gospel shine through. I wanted that audience to see that the gospel illuminates the way to be happy. My only purpose for being there was to help them come to the same realization I had: that what would get them through junior high and high school wasn't applause and popularity and recognition. It wasn't an unhealthy preoccupation with self-esteem, self-confidence, or self-love. In fact, it had so little to do with "self," and so much to do with Father in Heaven, that I could hardly stand it when it appeared that the youth were cheering for the wrong thing!

More than anything else, the simple principles I was taught each Sunday at church helped me survive my teenage years. That one day a week was more than enough to see me through the next six. What really got me through those years was the simple faith that God knew who I was and listened to my prayers. It was knowing that I could learn about him through my scriptures and my seminary classes. In recent years, I've realized how much my small but growing testimony guided my decisions back then. Even though at times I really felt awkward and alone, a tiny spark of faith inside told me that everything would be okay, and that I was going to make it.

And that's what I want to say to you in this little book. Of course, I'd much rather shake your hand and look you in the eye and say it to you in person, but I can't, so I'm going to use just a simple little phrase: *You're Gonna Make It.* You are. You're going to be fine. In fact, you'll be better than fine. You'll be amazing and wonderful and terrific. It may take some time, and you may have to be patient with yourself. You may even shed some tears from time to time. That's okay; I shed a few tears too when I was a teenager. But hang in there. You're gonna make it. You really are.

Together we'll learn that success in junior high and high school is not measured by how many times your picture appears in the yearbook, but by how you let the gospel map guide you safely and without regrets to graduation day. *The gospel* is what life is all about, and you're gonna make it because you have it. The gospel—now, *there's* something that deserves a standing ovation!

It took me from seventh grade to twelfth grade to catch on to these lessons even though I had been taught them all my life. Would you like to hear how I learned them? Okay— but first, go get a Slurpee. (You've been thinking about it, haven't you?) Then we'll go back in time and relive the "joys" of seventh grade. See you at roll call.

SEVENTH GRADE

Gee—What a Joy

The Lord will never forsake or abandon anyone. You may abandon him, but he will not abandon you. You never need feel that you are alone.

Elder Joseph B. Wirthlin
Ensign, November 1989, p. 75

J ust before I was to begin my seventh-grade year, my parents decided to move. It was not part of my plan. I had always thought I would go right into junior high with the friends I'd known since second grade, but it wasn't to be. It seemed like I was starting all over again, and I felt lost and lonely without my friends.

At my old elementary school, I had been student-body president. (I had also been the second-shortest boy in the sixth grade.) But now, going into seventh grade in a new school, a new neighborhood, a new situation, I was an unknown.

And my new school was so different! For one thing, everybody looked rich. Everything I wore came from the bargain basement table, and I felt like I'd walked into a fashion show. I hoped I would fit right in, but after a while it was clear that I was not going to retain my rung on the social ladder. I just didn't have the social skills or the wardrobe. I wanted to do all the things I had done before, to be involved in the activities and assemblies, but it wasn't going to happen. I didn't make the cut into the popular crowd. I don't know what crowd I was in. I guess I was just another number. I felt lost.

How did I make my grand entrance into Hillside Intermediate School? Well, when your name is "Bytheway," it's always a thrill. Just imagine—it's the first day of school. I'm sitting near the back of the room, waiting for the roll call. My last name starts with the second letter in the alphabet, so I know I'll be one of the first. The teacher will go through the A's, a few B's, and then she'll stop. Teachers always stop when they get to my name.

"Adams, Steve?"

"Here."

"Anderson, Stacey?"

"Here."

"Barlow, David?"

"Here."

"Brown, Amy?"

"Here."

Uh-oh. She stops. I knew it! She's looking at the roll differently—as if it's suddenly written in Chinese. She squints. Her forehead wrinkles with confusion. Her lips try to form the right sound. Finally, it comes out . . . will she get it right?

"Bith-way? Byth-way?"

"It's . . . it's Bytheway," my squeaky, not-yet-changed, seventh-grader voice says from the back of the room.

"Oh . . . By-the-way!"

She looks at the word again, and in a sudden stroke of genius realizes that you say it just the way it's spelled. Way to go, Einstein! Uh-oh, something else is happening. . . . Oh boy, it never fails. The wrinkled brow turns into a smile . . . here it comes . . . the teacher's going to make a joke . . . she just can't resist! *No one can ever resist!* It's the same joke all Bytheways have endured since the thirteenth century!

"Oh, by the way, John! Ha ha ha ha . . . "

The whole class snickers. I force a slight grin as everyone in the room turns to look at the new kid with the funny name. I can feel the blush moving up my face. Go on with the roll, *please!*

That was how the roll call went in every class except for one—in my gym class, Mr. Archibald pronounced it right. He said "Bytheway," and, of course, everybody laughed. But then Mr. Archibald looked up and said, "Hey, watch it! I married a Bytheway." (No wonder he got it right.)

After getting through roll call, another thing you have to do on the first day of school is pick someone to have a crush on. Even boys do that—at least I did. It wasn't hard for me. I walked into Miss Pratt's English class, and there was this beautiful blonde girl on the front row. As I went back to find a chair, she gave me the friendliest smile. I'll never forget that. I wondered if Pam—I found out her name during roll call—would smile at me like that every day. I figured anybody that pretty was probably out of my league, but, oh well. I could dream.

Certain parts of my daily routine did not exactly distinguish me as the big man on campus. Each day after English, I'd pick up my cornet (no, not a trumpet, a *cornet*—sounds like a female niblet), and carry it to band class. I looked like a really short traveling salesman with an over-sized suitcase. Now, we all know that band class is the cool place to be, right? Top of the totem pole, right?

Well, maybe not. But my band class was one of the things that helped me survive. I found a great group of people in there. They weren't the most popular or the most visible, but they were people like me who loved to make music. (I use the term *music* loosely—I mean, hey, we were seventh and eighth graders.) I also had a great band teacher, Mr. Baker, who took an interest in me. Thank heaven for great teachers.

Why am I telling you this? I call it "same-boat therapy." Too often, a teenager will feel as if he or she is the only one who has ever felt lost, alone, rejected, or misunderstood. Actually, all of us have felt like that from time to time. Everyone you know could tell you stories of feeling awkward and out of place. It's always nice to realize that someone else understands what you're going through.

Knowing that we've all been in the same boat doesn't really solve the problem or make the loneliness disappear, but doesn't it help just a little bit to know you're not alone? It doesn't? Oh. Uh-oh, now what do we do?

Let's try another approach. Let's try the gospel.

What do you do when you're lost? Let's say you're lost in the mall. (I know lots of people who would *love* to be lost in the mall—with a VISA card.) What do you do? You look for the Information sign that has that little map of all the stores, and then you look for the little red dot and the words "YOU ARE HERE." The map tells you exactly where you are and will help you figure out how to get where you want to go.

Even if you don't get lost very often in the mall, maybe sometimes you feel lost in life. Well, there's a map for that too. I have one. It's not the floor plan of a shopping mall—it's actually a map of time. It's called the *Wall Chart of World History*. It begins in about 4000 B.C. and goes all the way through time to about A.D. 1990. All together, it covers about 5990 years of time. When it's completely unfolded, it's about 13½ feet long—*over 13 feet!* That's a long chart, and it represents a long time. Just to put it in perspective, if you live to be 75 years old, your whole lifetime will be about 2 inches (right now, if you're a teenager, you've been alive for about ⅜ inch).

I'd love to show you my chart, but because we decided to print this book so it would fit on a shelf smaller than a Winnebago, we couldn't reproduce the chart here. Think about this, though: God could have sent you to earth anywhere within those 13½ feet. But he held you back so that you could come to earth in *the last half inch*. Thirteen feet, and you're here at the very end of the chart. What are the chances? Well, it's not by chance.

Here's what you need to know: The Lord had a specific

reason for sending you *here,* and sending you here *now.* Although you may feel lost, your Father in Heaven knows exactly who you are, where you are, and even "when" you are (see Acts 17:26).

As you know, a day to the Lord is a thousand years here on earth (see JST, 2 Peter 3:8). That's why we sometimes compare the earth's existence to a week: the first thousand years are like Monday, the next thousand like Tuesday, and so on. So, what day is it right now? Aha, this is where it gets exciting. Brace yourselves, folks—*it's Saturday night.* And guess who's coming first thing in the morning?

> *The Lord Jesus Christ is going to come "in the beginning of the seventh thousand years."* We, of course, cannot tell with certainty how many years passed from the fall of Adam to the birth of Jesus, nor whether the number of years counted by our present calendar has been tabulated without error. But *no one will doubt that we are in the Saturday night of time and that on Sunday morning the Lord will come.* (Bruce R. McConkie, *The Millennial Messiah* [Salt Lake City: Deseret Book, 1982], p. 31; emphasis added)

Perhaps the Primary song is speaking about more than just shining our shoes and washing our hair when it says, "Saturday is a special day. It's the day we get ready for Sunday"(*Children's Songbook,* p. 196).

Do you still think it's just an accident that you were born at the end of the chart? Think again! President Ezra Taft Benson said:

> You have been born at this time for a sacred and glorious purpose. It is not by chance that you have been reserved to come to earth in this last dispensation of the fulness of times. Your birth at this particular time was foreordained in the eternities. (*Ensign,* May 1986, p. 43)

Now do you see why I say the gospel can help you get through your teenage years better than any measure of popularity and recognition? No matter where you sit on the social ladder, no matter who your friends are, no matter what others say to you in the halls—or even if they ignore you—the message of the Lord and his prophets for you is constantly positive and reassuring. Your junior high experience is not a forecast for your life! You have a purpose, a mission, and a destiny to fulfill—a destiny that doesn't depend on your social status and your wardrobe. Whenever I pull out my 13-foot-long wall chart, I like to reread this amazing quote from President Ezra Taft Benson:

> For nearly six thousand years, God has held you in reserve to make your appearance in the final days before the second coming of the Lord. Every previous gospel dispensation has drifted into apostasy, but ours will not. . . . While our generation will be comparable in wickedness to the days of Noah, when the Lord cleansed the earth by flood, there is a major difference this time. It is that God has saved for the final inning some of his strongest children who will help bear off the kingdom triumphantly. And that is where you come in, for you are the generation that must be prepared to meet your God. All through the ages the prophets have looked down through the corridors of time to our day. Billions of the deceased and those yet to be born have their eyes upon us. Make no mistake about it—you are a marked generation. There has never been more expected of the faithful in such a short period of time as there is of us. Never before on the face of this earth have the forces of evil and the forces of good been as well organized. Now is the great day of the devil's power, with the greatest mass murderers of all time living among us. But now is also the great day of the

Lord's power, with the greatest number ever of priest-hood holders on the earth. And the showdown is fast approaching. ("In His Steps," *BYU Speeches of the Year, 1979* [Provo, Utah: BYU Press, 1980], p. 59)

My friend, you are *not* lost. You were sent here on purpose as one of God's strongest children. You must be somebody special. I mean, it's obvious. Think about it—what are you doing *right now?* You're reading a Church book! How many teenagers do you think are doing *that* right now? Not many! (Your Honor, I offer this as Exhibit "A" that the person reading this book is way beyond average.)

So if you're feeling lonely, it's okay. Hang in there. Do you think any of us can teach Jesus anything about being lonely or unpopular or misunderstood? He knows. He really knows. And that means he knows exactly how to help us. Remember, Jesus took upon himself not only our sins but also all our pains and afflictions and sorrows.

And he shall go forth, suffering pains and afflictions and temptations of *every kind;* and this that the word might be fulfilled which saith he will take upon him the pains and the sicknesses of his people. (Alma 7:11; emphasis added)

Did you notice the words "every kind"? Is "every" a pretty high percentage? Yes it is. He knows what you're going through!

President Boyd K. Packer said:

What a wonderful time to be young. You will see events in your lifetime that will test your courage and extend your faith. If you will face the sunlight of truth [not the eclipses of popularity], the shadows of discouragement and sin and error will fall behind you. You must never give up! . . .

God bless you young women and young men who struggle through the worrisome teenage years. Some of you may not yet have found yourselves, but *you are not lost,* for Jesus is the Christ, the Son of God, our Savior and Redeemer. (*Ensign,* May 1989, p. 59; emphasis added)

Yes, I began my sojourn through junior high school feeling lost. But Heavenly Father knew exactly where I was. And he knows where you are too. For me, seventh grade was such a "joy." Actually, it was hard, but I'm so glad that I had the gospel to help me. I had the scriptures and the prophets to continually remind me that if I would stay close to my Father in Heaven, I could handle anything school could throw at me. Deep, deep down, I knew things would be okay. I hope you feel that way too. Let these words ring in your ears: *You are not lost, and you're gonna make it!*

Join me next chapter, and I'll tell you how the gospel helped me through the toughest school year of my whole life.

EIGHTH GRADE

I Don't Think There Are Words Adequate to Describe Eighth Grade

It was meant to be that life would be a challenge. To suffer some anxiety, some depression, some disappointment, even some failure is normal.

Teach our members that if they have a good, miserable day once in a while, or several in a row, to stand steady and face them. Things will straighten out.

There is great purpose in our struggle in life.

Elder Boyd K. Packer
Ensign, May 1978, p. 93

My institute teacher friend A. David Thomas once said, "If you can make it through eighth grade, you can make it through anything." That was certainly true for me. Eighth grade was my hardest year—and as you've probably already guessed, when I say "hard," I'm not talking about the classes and the teachers and the grades. Those were the easy parts.

Some of the saddest things I've ever seen happened at my junior high school. These years can be a time of over-powering insecurity. You worry about your clothes, your body shape, and your social status. Every message you get from the world tells you that these are the ways to measure your worth: if you don't have the right clothes, the attrac-tive or athletic "bod," and the right group to hang out with, then you are somehow second-class. Sometimes it seems there are daily attacks on your feelings about yourself.

I remember standing in the library one day when a pop-ular girl came to the front desk to check out some books. She looked at the short-haired student helper and asked loudly, "Are you a boy or a girl?" Ouch. You could have heard a pin drop. The student librarian was a girl, and a friend of mine. I'll never forget watching her barely get out the words "I'm a girl" before she walked away and started to cry. I felt so bad for her.

Other attacks that can result in a lot of hidden sadness and embarrassment occur at school dances. Besides that group who seem to dance every dance, there's always another group who rarely get asked, and others who spend the first two hours of the dance just trying to get up the courage to ask, only to be coldly turned down. One girl decided she really didn't want to dance with the boy who had asked her, so during the middle of the song, when he turned his back for a moment, she ran away. How do you suppose this young man felt when he turned around and his partner was gone? What message did she send to him? Ouch again!

There are also people who get mercilessly teased. You know exactly what I'm talking about, don't you! You've seen it at your school. Teasing, unfortunately, is often aimed at something over which we have no control—our height, our size, some physical feature. And because we can't do anything about it, we might think it will never change, and that hurts even worse.

Some young people walk home so emotionally bloodied and beat up after a day of school that it's hard for them to have any desire to go back the next day and face it all over again. What can you do if school feels like an ordeal? You want to be liked, you want to matter, but you can't seem to find where you fit in.

Go Away!

Before we get into specifics, let me tell you something that happened to me in eighth grade that changed my perspective. It all took place in my science class. Each day, before we went to our individual tables with our lab partners, our teacher would give the whole class a lecture, kind of an "opening exercises." One day, the teacher mentioned a scientific principle I had heard the day before on the TV show *Hogan's Heroes.* No sooner did I recall this idea than a boy named Steve—the student-body president and someone I had long admired but never spoken to—raised his hand and made the same comment I was about to make.

As we were dismissed to go to our lab tables, I got up the nerve to talk to Steve. I said, "You watched *Hogan's*

Heroes yesterday, huh." He smiled and said "yeah" as he walked to his lab table. I was excited that he had talked to me and that he had been nice. A moment later, one of his lab partners walked over to me and asked, very sarcastically, "Oh, do you want to be in our group?" All I could do was look at him in silence. Finally I softly said "no," and he walked away.

I got his message loud and clear: *Go away. Don't step out of your social group and try to talk to someone in another group.* While they went to their lab table and laughed and joked and did the experiments, I sat down with my lab partner, a quiet boy who was legally blind, and we started going through the workbook.

My mind was racing as I sat down. What was all this about? Things had been so different where I used to live. All of a sudden, school wasn't about spelling tests and math problems; it was about being with the right people, wearing the right clothes, being involved in the right activities. It was about being one of the few to have your romance mentioned in the school paper. And if you weren't one of the popular crowd, then the game was locked, and nobody else could play. You were a loner, a loser, a wanna-be. Your job was to watch all the others do the fun things in the assemblies, write the school paper, and be habitually late for classes because they got to participate in special leadership field trips and retreats and meetings. Your job was to hear about all the parties and activities to which you weren't invited. The only thing you *could* do was wish you were one of them. But that was as far as you could go, because they were very good at drawing boundaries.

This "go away" incident had a major impact on my life. The truth was, yes, I did want to be in their group. At least I had wanted to until that moment. Suddenly I realized that this brand of popularity was *not* something to be admired.

As I sat there, I thought to myself, "I don't want to be like that." The guy who was rude to me was high on the popularity totem pole, but that day my respect for him hit rock bottom. I guess this was the first time I realized that there is a big difference between being *respected* and being *popular.* At that moment, I cared much less about being popular, and I cared much more about being respected. I think it's much better to be respected, don't you? Popularity ends on yearbook day, but respect lasts forever.

Popularity or Respect?

Fortunately, some of the popular students were also nice. One day I was walking down the hall to go to lunch, and this really nice guy said, "Hey, John!" My first thought was, *How does he know my name?* He went on, "Hey, John, do you want to go to lunch?" "Sure," I responded, and Richard and I sat down and ate lunch together in the cafeteria. He also took time to introduce me to some of his friends as they walked by. Now, *this* was something I could admire. He was popular, no question about it. But he also won my respect. He liked people, and people liked him because he was nice to everybody.

All of this taught me to view popularity in the proper perspective. If we're not careful, we may spend all our school years trying to climb the ladder of social success, only to find that the ladder was leaning against the wrong wall! The proper wall to lean it against is labeled *respect.* The Church's pamphlet *For the Strength of Youth* says, "Treat everyone with kindness and dignity" (p. 9). Concentrate on being respectful to others, and you'll be respected. And who knows, maybe you'll be popular, too.

If you're already in the popular group, good for you! Maybe you serve in student government; maybe you're an athlete or a cheerleader. Make that monogrammed sweater or letterman's jacket mean something! Don't let it be a sign that says, "Go away!" Make it an *invitation* that says, "Come and talk to me! How are your classes going? Don't we have a great school? Anything I can do to help?" If you're a leader in your school, you're in a great position to lift and help and inspire others. You'll be able to use that position and status to show the world how we should treat one another, and others will follow your lead. Don't miss this great opportunity to set a powerful example!

If we don't invite people into our circle, some other group will invite them into theirs. Speaking of those who are lonely and struggling, Sister Joy F. Evans said: "They will find friends somewhere; they will find comfort somewhere. What is our failure if they find it elsewhere because we were not there, were not welcoming?" (*Ensign,* May 1989, p. 74.) She's right! If we say "go away" to those who need our help, they may someday say "go away" to us when we try to rescue them from the wrong crowd, or drugs, or gangs. Even worse, they might say "go away" when we try to share the gospel with them with our words, a gospel that they couldn't recognize in our actions. Don't let it happen!

Well, we've decided to focus on being respected and respectful, and that's nice, but let's face it: Life is still tough. What else can we do? I wish I had a real earth-shaking, incredible answer to wipe out all your problems, but I don't. In fact, I'm afraid that what I say might be kind of a disappointment, but it's all I've got. Here it is: Hang in there, keep going, be patient with yourself, and don't give up. Did that help? It didn't? Uh-oh. Now what do we do? Just like last chapter, I guess we'd better turn to the gospel.

No Wonder You Don't See Yourself Right: You're Looking in the Wrong Mirror!

The world sends us all kinds of different and sometimes false messages, but the gospel is consistent and crystal

clear. Brother Stephen R. Covey compared the messages
we get from the world to a mirror (see *The Divine Center*
[Salt Lake City: Bookcraft, 1982], pp. 162–63). Not just any
mirror, but the crazy mirrors we see at carnivals or at the
"fun house." We laugh at those distorted reflections. Why?
Because we know they are not true.

Think about this: what if the *only* information you had
about how you looked came from a fun-house mirror? If
that was the only reflection you had, you'd honestly believe
that that was how you looked! What if, after you had spent
years seeing your reflection in that fun-house mirror, somebody suddenly held a true and correct mirror in front of you
and revealed to you who you really were? Wouldn't that be
a shock?

A wonderful mom and friend of mine called me one day
and asked if I could help her daughter, who was having
some trouble with her friends at school. Thinking of
Brother Covey's mirror idea, I wanted to let the girl know
that she had three *true mirrors* in her life: her family, her
true friends, and her Heavenly Father. They were the only
ones who could be trusted to reflect her real value. Finally,
I wrote it as a poem to Kerry Lynne:

Mirrors

*Did you ever go up to the fun house to play, and look in
    the mirrors there?*
*They bend up your face, and widen your waist, and alter
    the shape of your hair.*
*In one place you're as huge as a hot-air balloon, in
    another as thin as a stick,*
*At first you're as slim as a telephone pole, and everywhere
    else, you are thick.*
*Some people are mirrors reflecting to us an image we
    really are not;*
If we think that those mirrors are telling the truth, we've

been blinded to all that we've got.
Some say that we're ornery or stupid or weird, some say
that we're stuck-up or fat,
But in others you'll view a reflection of you that doesn't
have any of that.
Who are the best mirrors that you and I have? Who gives a
reflection that's true?
Who sees us for all that is hidden inside? Your Father in
Heaven, that's who.
You've also got teachers and parents and friends whose
reflections are true and correct;
When peers say you're homely or haughty or dumb, God
says, "You're my child, you're elect."
So get out some paper, and pick up a pen, and write down
what others may say,
Then turn the page over, and fill it with things the Lord and
the prophets convey.
On one side you'll have all that others have said: some are
true, some are hard to conceive;
Then turn to God's side, and ask of yourself, Which side
am I going to believe?

Once again, we see that the gospel mirror is the best thing to see us through our junior high and high school trials. I had the same great mirrors when I was in school: my true friends, my family, and my Heavenly Father.

True Friends

Elder Robert D. Hales defined a true friend as one who "makes it easier for us to live the gospel by being around him [or her]. . . . A true friend does not make us choose between his way and the Lord's way" (*Ensign,* May 1990, p. 40). Such true friends make true mirrors.

I'll never forget the day I attended my first meeting in our new ward. One of the young men, a guy named Mike Schauerhamer (pronounced "Shower-hammer"—we often teased each other about our last names), was the first to welcome me into the ward. I will never forget his kindness. He must have repeated four or five times, "We really want you to feel welcome." That's pretty impressive for an eighth grader.

My friends in my ward were true mirrors for me. Whatever happened to me at school, I could count on my friends in the Parley's Second Ward. I hope your ward is that way. If not, do what you can to "be like Mike" (Mike Schauerhamer, I mean). Of all the places in the world, your ward is one place where there shouldn't be any cliques! President Gordon B. Hinckley counseled:

> Thank you for your strength. Thank you for your goodness. Thank you for your courage. Thank you for your efforts in hanging together, as it were, of going to institute, going to seminary, partaking of the blessings that are to be had there, not only in the teaching of the gospel but in society in which you can mingle. I want to say to you, look for your friends among the members of the Church, band together and strengthen one another. And when the time of temptation comes you will have someone to lean on to bless you and give you strength when you need it. That is what this Church is for—so that we can help one another in our times of weakness to stand on our feet tall and straight and true and good. (*Church News,* March 1, 1997, p. 2)

To this day I'm grateful for the friends in my ward who stuck by me. Only in recent years have I realized what a great blessing and protection that was. Good, true friends can be a powerful influence to keep you on the right track.

What if things are a little sparse in the friendship department? Well, there are other mirrors. Some teens don't know that. Unfortunately, many consider their peer group as the one and only mirror, the only source of information about who they are and what they're worth! If your whole world revolves around what your peers think, you're in for a trip that will make Space Mountain look like a two-mile-per-hour stroller ride.

In September of 1995, President Hinckley announced the Church's "Proclamation on the Family." Notice that the Church did not announce a "Proclamation on Your Peers." We're not going to get into that kind of a fickle festival. Remember the definition of good friends, and we'll move over and take a closer look into the family mirror.

Your Family

Although my family wasn't perfect, I always knew I was welcome there. Sure, there were times when we didn't get along perfectly, but when the chips were down, I always knew I could count on "the fam." I'll never forget the times we would kneel around Mom and Dad's bed and have family prayer together. Somehow it seemed as if someone would always say something really funny just before we all knelt down. Dad would kneel at the end of the bed and try to maintain his fatherly composure while considering who he should call on. Finally he'd say someone's name and then bust out laughing. That triggered a domino effect. One by one we'd all start laughing, and it would take a few minutes to get everybody serious enough to pray. (I hate to admit this, so I'll put it in parentheses—sometimes the bed would start to wiggle during the prayer, and we knew someone was laughing again. In my heart of hearts, I believe that on some of those occasions, Heavenly Father was laughing too—or at least smiling.)

I love the story that my friend Brad Wilcox tells about his parents. When he was in seventh grade, he found out that it wasn't cool to love your parents, so he tried to hate them. He says that it wasn't as easy as he first thought to hate his parents, because he really loved them. But "a man's gotta do what a man's gotta do." One day, Brad was climbing over a fence in his backyard. As he tells it:

> Suddenly, the barbed wire on which I was balancing gave out. I landed forcefully on the fence, and the jagged wooden post shot through my right hand—yes, in one side and out the other. Believe me, my first thought was not *I hate my parents.* I began yelling for my mom and dad as loudly as I could. . . . My dad was driving up the driveway. He heard me screaming and rushed to the fence. He pulled my hand off the post, wrapped it in a dish towel, and hurried me to the hospital emergency room. Not once did I think, *I can't stand this guy. He doesn't like my music. He doesn't like my hair.* Not once did I think, *I am going to be so embarrassed if any of my friends see me with my dad.* . . . The entire time the doctor stitched my right hand back together, my dad sat next to me, holding my left hand and squeezing it over and over. I'll never forget the love I felt from my dad that day—the very day I had decided I was going to hate him. (In Randal A. Wright, ed., *Friends Forever* [Salt Lake City: Bookcraft, 1996], pp. 25–26)

If you have a mom and/or dad that you can really talk to, I think tonight you should fall to your knees and thank your Heavenly Father for that blessing. Your family can really help and support you during these teenage years. I know young people who say their parents are their best friends! That's great. I didn't talk much about some things to my parents, but I know it was my fault, not theirs. I think they would have been very willing to listen, but I was too embarrassed, so I kept most of my problems to myself. (I guess they can read this if they want to know what junior high was like for me.)

Sometimes we don't talk to our parents because we think they don't know how we feel. Often our parents—the people who love us the very most—try so hard to encourage us, and we don't listen! Have you ever heard this from your mom or dad: "You're neat!" "You're special!" "You can do it!" And what do we do? We roll our eyes and say, "Oh, Mom." We think to ourselves, "They don't understand." We think that just because they don't know the jargon, they don't know the feelings, either. But seriously, what if your mother came running into your room and said, "Dude, whassup?! You rock my world!" You probably wouldn't listen to her then, either. You'd say, "Mom, stop trying to be a teenager."

Please be very careful about the way you treat your family. There is no commandment that says, "Honor thy friends," but there is one that says, "Honour thy father and thy mother" (Exodus 20:12). And if you look at the footnote accompanying the word *honour,* it says, "Respect, or Value."

Although most of us can trust the mirrors our parents hold up for us, there are, unfortunately, always exceptions. I have met teenagers who come from very difficult family situations, from families torn apart by alcoholism, abuse, divorce, and more. But even these young people have another mirror in which to look.

Your Heavenly Father

There really isn't anything you can tell your Heavenly Father that will surprise him. He knows exactly what you are going through. It's nice to know that.

I remember hearing, early in my eighth-grade year, that a notorious bully in the school wanted to fight me. I won't tell you his name, but he had the same last name as a famous boxer. How comforting. I had no desire to fight him. I don't know what I did to receive this honor. I didn't even know him! Maybe it was his way of making new students feel welcome. What was his problem? Why did he care?

Aren't you supposed to dislike people before you fight them? I just didn't get it. But, far be it from me to question the rules of eighth-grade life.

Anyway, I didn't know what to do. But I did know that the gospel was where I should turn for help. I was too embarrassed to tell my parents, but I knew who I *could* tell: my Father in Heaven. He knew all about it, and he would know what to do.

By this time, I had learned a few things at church about how to get answers to prayer. First of all, you made yourself really hungry. (We call it "fasting," although it ought to be called "slowing" because it seems to make time move a lot slower.) I also knew that you were supposed to pray for your enemies. So I did. I asked the Lord to "soften his heart" toward me. I didn't want to be a coward, so I went to school, I walked down the same halls as always, and I followed my same routine.

Was I scared? Yes, I was. I had seen this kid beat other people up and hit them while they were down. I don't know how the world produces people like that, but it does. I really wanted to go home with the same number of teeth I had come to school with. Whenever I felt hunger pangs, I would remember why I was fasting, and I'd say another little prayer. I knew I would run into him sooner or later.

Finally, the inevitable confrontation came. I saw him coming toward me down "A" hall (each hall at Hillside has a letter). I kept walking. He stopped. He said, "Hey, Bytheway, how ya doin'?" Then I stopped. "Fine," I answered. We kept talking. I can't remember what he said, but I remember that he was looking at me differently. It was almost as if he were intimidated. He was really nice!

What happened? To this day I have no earthly idea. Did somebody tell him I was a karate champ? Did someone tell him I could bench-press a bus? Did one of the Three

Nephites visit him? I don't know. I may never know. I'm so curious! Maybe the Lord will tell me someday. Whatever caused it, this event turned out to be one of my most faith-building spiritual experiences.

Many years later, I received my patriarchal blessing. It would be inappropriate to share any specifics, but when the patriarch told me that the Lord had watched over me from time to time, this incident came into my mind, and I knew it was true. God had watched over me. I knew he had.

Thank heaven for true mirrors. Maybe, for whatever reason, it's hard for you to talk to your parents about things. I'd encourage you to try. But in the meantime, remember this: "God knows the feelings in every human heart. He can soften sorrow and lead when there seems to be no light. . . . If all else fails, remember: God and one other person can be a family" (Marvin J. Ashton, *Ensign,* May 1988, p. 64).

You've heard tons of quotations about who you are and what responsibilities you have in the latter days. I believe in you, because I know you believe in God. He sent you here for a reason, and he believes in you too. He loves you. And God and one other person can be a family.

Sometimes we try to solve our problems on our own, not realizing the power of the Lord to help us. We're like a little kid who has a sliver in his finger that hurts so badly he won't let anyone else see it. And when someone tries to help him remove it, he won't hold still! Well, I learned a lesson in eighth grade that I've learned over and over again ever since: you do the best you can, and then you stand still and let God do the rest. He is so powerful.

While imprisoned in Liberty Jail, the Prophet Joseph Smith wrote a letter to the Saints about the persecutions they had suffered. This is his closing paragraph: "Therefore, dearly beloved brethren, let us cheerfully do all things that lie in our power; and then may we stand still, with the utmost assurance, to see the salvation of God, and for his arm to be revealed" (Doctrine and Covenants 123:17).

A Few Closing Thoughts

So what do you do if everywhere you go, you seem to get the message, "Go away!" You get it in the hall, you get it in the cafeteria, you get it on the way home, you seem to get it from everyone at school. What do you do?

Well, I noticed something in the scriptures the other day that I thought was incredible. It even used the words *go away.* I couldn't believe it! Jesus often told us to follow his example, to do what he did. Well, this time, he seemed to be saying, "Did you notice that I *never* said this? You saw that, didn't you?" So if you ever feel like the whole world seems to be telling you, "Go away; you're not in our group," I want you to remember this: "And ye see that I have commanded that none of you should go away, but rather have commanded that ye should come unto me, that ye might feel and see" (3 Nephi 18:25). Jesus never said "go away." His words were always an invitation.

Nephi knew all about this. He wrote:

> Behold, doth he cry unto any, saying: Depart from me? Behold, I say unto you, Nay; but he saith: Come unto me all ye ends of the earth, buy milk and honey, without money and without price.
>
> Behold, hath he commanded any that they should depart out of the synagogues, or out of the houses of worship? Behold, I say unto you, Nay.
>
> Hath he commanded any that they should not partake of his salvation? Behold I say unto you, Nay; but he hath given it free for all men; and he hath commanded his people that they should persuade all men to repentance.

> Behold, hath the Lord commanded any that they should not partake of his goodness? Behold I say unto you, Nay; but all men are privileged the one like unto the other, and none are forbidden. (2 Nephi 26:25–28)

Once again, we see that the gospel can help us through anything. It doesn't remove the problems, but it helps us get through them (see Helaman 5:12). Do you still have some eighth-grade type problems? Me too. We all do. But now we know where to go. In eighth grade or any grade, the answer is to come to Jesus (see Matthew 11:28). His invitation still stands, and he wants us to be in "his group."

Well, there's more of school to go through. Oh goodie. Thanks for sticking with it, and I'll see you in ninth grade!

NINTH GRADE

What Can I Be?

Use what talents you possess: the woods would be very silent if no birds sang except those that sang best.

Henry Van Dyke

Well, I made it through eighth grade, and that meant I was off to high school. (Grades nine through twelve were all together at my high school.) So I showed up at Highland High with my cornet. There were a few adjustments to make. The halls were so long, and there were so many classrooms, and the building seemed gigantic. Along with my cornet, I brought along many ninth-grader concerns: What if I couldn't make it from one end of the school to the other before the bell rang? What if I had to ask somebody how to find a room and they told me the wrong place on purpose? What if a senior locked me inside my locker? What if my lunch box wasn't cool? (Just kidding—I *knew* my lunch box was cool.) Everything was new and different. And some of the students! Wow, they were huge! They looked like . . . like . . . adults! There were guys who *shaved,* and some of the students drove cars to school! Incredible. I told my cornet, "Toto, I have a feeling we're not in Kansas anymore." (The spooky thing is, my cornet used to talk back.)

Another thing I began to notice was that some of these students were really good at things. I heard seniors singing in the music rooms, and they had that wavy thing in their voices we call "vibrato." I saw student athletes in track, football, and basketball who were strong and skilled and talented. I saw drawings in the showcase done by some of the art students, and they were excellent. I saw nice-looking furniture on display that students had made in wood shop.

Seeing all of these achievements made me wonder—what can I do? What can I be? Like lots of ninth graders, I didn't feel like I could do anything. I mean, I could do lots of things, but I wasn't really good at anything. I wanted to be good at something!

Back in eighth grade, I knew a student named Joe who seemed to be a fairly average kid. One day someone told me he was the number-four tennis player for his age-group in the intermountain area. I looked at him differently after that. Wouldn't you? I think when we find out that somebody does something really well, our respect for that person increases. And I think our self-respect may increase, too, when we work at a talent or a hobby.

It's really nice to have something you can do well, something that gives you satisfaction. In fact, I'd like to recommend to you that you find something you're good at and then work hard at it. (TV watching doesn't count.) This reminds me of a story I once heard about Brigham Young that I'll never forget.

An English writer with a great respect for titles wrote a letter to Brigham Young, addressing it "To His Excellency, Brigham Young, Governor of the Territory of Utah, President of the Church of Jesus Christ of Latter-day Saints, Indian Agent of the Territory."

When they met, President Young told the man he'd omitted one of his titles.

"Do you mean the generalship, Governor?" the writer asked.

"No, no. I mean, Brigham Young, master cabinetmaker, painter and glazier," said the Church President (as told by Steve Hale, *Ensign,* May 1971, p. 47).

How interesting! Go look up "Brigham Young" in the encyclopedia; I doubt it will say, "Brigham Young: a great cabinetmaker," but that was one of the ways Brigham

Young thought of himself. I'll bet amidst all the pressures of his many leadership roles, he loved to be by himself in his workshop making things.

How about you? What can you do? Any ideas? I bet we could find things you could do for every letter of the alphabet. Ready? How about archery, basketball, composing, drawing, exercise, football, golf, hiking, ice skating, jogging, kick soccer, listening, mowing, needlepoint, observing, piano playing, quilting, reading, singing, track and field, understanding, visiting, writing, xylophone, yodeling, and zoo! Okay, so some of them are a little lame, and some don't end in "-ing," but you get the point. Elder Marvin J. Ashton said:

> One of the great tragedies of life, it seems to me, is when a person classifies himself as someone who has no talents or gifts. When, in disgust or discouragement, we allow ourselves to reach depressive levels of despair because of our demeaning self-appraisal, it is a sad day for us and a sad day in the eyes of God. For us to conclude that we have no gifts when we judge ourselves by stature, intelligence, grade-point average, wealth, power, position, or external appearance is not only unfair but unreasonable. . . . It is up to each of us to search for and build upon the gifts which God has given. We must remember that each of us is made in the image of God, that there are no unimportant persons. (*Ensign,* November 1987, p. 20)

If you feel as if you are lacking in talents or gifts, please remember that you are very young, and it might take some time to find out what you can do well. Many of us will try many different things and even fail at many different things before we find something we really love. But all of us have the capacity to do something right now. Let's go back to our alphabetical list for a second, and let's focus on "L" and

"U"—listening and understanding. Folks, we have a short-age in those areas. Our world needs more people who are good at those things. If you're at a loss for what you can be, then "listen" and "understand" this story from Sister Patricia Holland:

> When my daughter, Mary, was just a small child, she was asked to perform a talent for a PTA contest. This is her experience exactly as she wrote it in her seven-year-old script:
>
> "I was practicing the piano one day and it made me cry because it was bad. Then I decided to practice bal-let, and it made me cry more—it was bad too. So then I decided to draw a picture because I knew I could do that good, but it was horrid. Of course it made me cry.
>
> "Then my little three-year-old brother came up and I said, 'Duffy, what *can* I be? What can *I* be? I can't be a piano player or an artist or a ballet girl. What can I be?' He came up to me and whispered, 'You can be my sister.'"
>
> In an important moment, those five simple words changed the perspective and comforted the heart of a very anxious child. Life became better right on the spot and, as always, tomorrow was a brighter day. (*On Earth as it is in Heaven* [Salt Lake City: Deseret Book, 1989], p. 3)

Making a difference in the world may begin by making a difference in our families. We need more teenagers who will say in their hearts, "I am a world-class, All-American, gold-medal, top-ten big brother or big sister." Now, I know some of you might be saying, "Oh, great. I can be good at something that doesn't matter. Oooh, be careful what you say! It *does* matter to be a good brother or sister. It matters a lot. In fact, the day will come when you realize that the most important roles we have in this life involve our relationships with our families. Anyway, we need more listeners and understanders. You can be that right away—tonight! Then you can start working on some other things, too.

Back in ninth grade, I really wasn't sure what I could do. I'd been trying to play the cornet since the sixth grade, but I was beginning to lose interest (the same way I lost interest in playing the piano—two things I really regret today). I didn't know what I could do. Fortunately, God was watching over me (and he's watching over you too).

Intersections and Happy Accidents

A few years ago I saw a poster that said, "In Michigan in 1898 there were only two automobiles: they collided." What luck! In the whole state there were only two cars, and they ran into each other. We call that an accident.

The most likely place for an automobile accident to occur is in an intersection. But some intersections are no accident. You will "collide" with other people throughout your life, and some of those collisions may actually have been arranged for your growth.

On Freshman Orientation Day at Highland High School, I attended an assembly where I saw three short-skirted young women and three hyper young men who yelled and cheered and jumped up and down a lot. They seemed to be really gung ho about school spirit. After that, I went to register for my classes. A bunch of teachers were sitting at tables around the outer edge of the gym. If you wanted to be in a particular class, you'd take a little card from that teacher's table, and you'd hand in your seven cards when you were done. After getting the required English and math courses, I had one elective to choose, and I was really excited. I had been looking over several selections, but Architectural Drawing seemed the most interesting to me. When I asked for a card, the man said, "I'm sorry, I'm all full. Why don't you take Commercial Art instead?" Obedient little ninth grader that I was, I picked up a card for Commercial Art.

I didn't realize it at the time, but this was a happy accident—a great intersection in my life. I'm so glad that teacher recommended another class instead of just saying his own class was full. I had always liked to draw, but now I "collided" with a great art teacher, Harold A. Peterson, who taught me and inspired me and over the next four years helped me find something that I could be.

President Spencer W. Kimball once said, "God does love us, and he watches over us. But it is usually through another person that he meets our needs." In this case, the other person was a teacher at the school. In other cases, it might be adults you see on a weekly basis: your Sunday School teacher, your Young Men's or Young Women's advisor, your bishop. The Church is an amazing organization, and it has all of the ordinances we need for salvation, but there's more to it than that. The prophet Moroni mentioned other reasons for us to meet together: "And the church did meet together oft, to fast and to pray, and to speak one with another concerning the welfare of their souls" (Moroni 6:5).

If I could take a moment to give you some brotherly advice, I'd tell you to make friends not only with the youth in your ward but with the adults too. They can help you with so many intersections. They can steer you in the right direction and warn you when it's time to put on the brakes.

I'll never forget Brother John Peay, one of my advisors who helped me through my teenage years. Every week he would ask us, "How's it going?" And he really wanted to know. Like the members in Moroni's time, he was speaking with us "concerning the welfare of our souls." I had many long talks with Brother Peay. He helped me with my feelings of insecurity; he counseled me about the girls I wanted to meet; he even took me on fishing trips where we talked about all kinds of things in between the big ones that got away. He wasn't just my leader; he was my friend.

Thank heaven for adult leaders. I hope you'll take advantage of having these advisors who are literally "at your service" every week. They're called *advisors,* so let them advise! They're not telling you what to do, they're telling you how to be happy! I've been tempted to say, "If you think there's a big generation gap, maybe it's the one between your ears," but, of course, I would never say that. Get over yourself, and go make friends with your leaders. It may just be that Heavenly Father put your advisors there for a reason—to help you. A brilliant teenager like yourself will realize that whether or not they speak your language or listen to your music, they might know some things you haven't yet learned! They might have some great advice on how to be happier and make wiser choices about the future.

One of the greatest things about the Church is that it gives us intersections—opportunities to meet other people whom the Lord can use to help meet our needs. Elder Neal A. Maxwell said, "Just as the rising generation is here, now, by divine design—so are we who have been placed just ahead of them. Our lives and theirs have and will intersect many times before it is all over, and not by accident" (*Ensign,* April 1985, p. 11).

An Hour a Day, That's All We Ask

Another happy intersection in my ninth-grade year was right across the street from school. I ran into a red brick building with a very familiar title on the side: *The Church of Jesus Christ of Latter-day Saints.* Growing up where I did, I had the opportunity of attending "released-time" seminary during one of the regular class periods of the school day. (It wasn't until later that I learned about the wonderful, valiant youth around the country who participate in "early-morning" or home-study seminary.) Seminary was the bright spot in my day. This was a place where I seemed to know a few more answers, where I always felt comfortable. When I was introduced to my seminary teacher, Brother Swanson, I remember thinking, "This guy is one of the happiest, most energetic people I've ever seen in my life." He was so enthusiastic about the gospel. I wondered from time to time if *I* knew the gospel was true, but there was no doubt in my mind that Brother Swanson knew. I don't know what Brother Swanson saw in me, but he asked me to be seminary class president. This was the first school-related leadership position I'd had since sixth grade.

On one occasion, Brother Swanson planned a testimony meeting. He tried everything he possibly could to bring the Spirit into the room. A hymn was playing as we entered; he spoke in softer tones; he asked us to be reverent. Unfortunately, some of the students had the idea that seminary was kind of like free time to mess around. After the meeting, which hadn't been as successful as he had hoped, Brother Swanson looked at the floor and talked with his class president about what had happened. It was kind of like he was talking to himself and I just happened to be there to hear. He said something like, "I just wanted this meeting to work out so much. I wanted them to feel the Spirit." Something changed inside me as I watched his disappointment. I knew that this was really important to him, that he wasn't just there to do his job and then go home. He really cared about the Lord, about teaching, and about us. I don't think I ever told Brother Swanson what an impact he had on me. I think I should. I should also thank Heavenly Father for that intersection.

I Was Fifteen Goin' On . . .

In ninth grade, I watched a lot of people do things that I wanted to do. But I was kind of, well, timid. I had been stomped on before for trying to leave "my group," and I didn't like it. Like most ninth graders, I still battled the feelings of not belonging, of wondering what I could be. When I opened the yearbook at the end of my ninth-grade year, I turned to the same spot you and I always turn to first—our own picture. I leafed through pages highlighting the extracurricular activities: the music, the drama, the sports, and the honor clubs. Among all the pages of photos of people who seemed to know what they could be, I finally found my single, solitary photo in the rather unexciting section titled "Freshmen."

It took me years to see that the difficult things I went through in junior high and high school were actually good for me. One of the hardest things to say to a teenager—and one of the hardest things for a teenager to hear—is this little two-word phrase: "Be patient." It took me years to realize that Heavenly Father knew what he was doing, and that I could "be still, and know" that he was God. One poet said it like this:

My life is but a weaving, between my God and me,
I do not choose the colors, He worketh steadily,
Ofttimes He weaveth sorrow, and I in foolish pride,
Forget He sees the upper, and I the underside.
Not till the loom is silent, and shuttles cease to fly,
Will God unroll the canvas and explain the reason why.
The dark threads are as needful in the skillful Weaver's
    hand,
As the threads of gold and silver in the pattern He has
    planned.
("The Weaver," in Book of Poetry, *ed. Al Bryant [New York:*
    Zondervan Publishing House, 1968])

Someone once said that a blessing is anything that moves us closer to God. I could not honestly say that I enjoyed much about the years from seventh to ninth grade. Looking back now, however, I'm kind of glad that I was not included in the popular loop, that I was a bit of a loner for a while. During those times, God gave me a heart. I would not soon forget how it felt to be a teenager—in fact, I think I'll be able to remember those feelings for a long, long time. I'm glad about that, because, among other things, it means I get to talk to you. So listen up, friend, 'cause I'm here to tell you something. *You're gonna make it.* You really are. Hang in there! Stay close to the Lord, and whatever you do, don't give up.

Well, things got a little worse before they got better. Stick with me, and I'll give you the details of my next big trial. (It has to do with something that kept showing up on my face.) Have a nice summer, and I'll see you in tenth grade.

TENTH GRADE

Getting Is Not As Good As Becoming

As you review the last year or the last ten years, what is the best day you remember? A person without hope centered in Christ may choose a day that was simply fun or easy. But the best day may really have been the one when life's events forced you to your knees to communicate with your Father with new intent; it may have been a day that wasn't convenient or even happy, but you became a bigger and better person when you faced a problem with courage.

Sister Dwan J. Young
Ensign, November 1986, p. 87

Perhaps one of the most difficult aspects of my teenage life peaked during my sophomore year. I developed acne. (I was going to say it "came to a head" during my sophomore year, but I thought that was not the best choice of words.) Among all the other insecurities teenagers deal with, it seems completely unfair that acne gets added to everything else. I began to notice the problem in about seventh grade, and it became steadily worse with time. I would get blemishes all over my face and back. I didn't mind them on my back as much, because they were hidden from view. But, as any acne sufferer knows, the last thing you need when you have acne is a "pat on the back." Ouch.

Acne was incredibly frustrating for me. It caused me to withdraw from certain social situations because I was too embarrassed. I even stayed home from school on some days and just did my work at home because I did not want to be seen. I'll bet I single-handedly kept Stridex and Clearasil in business. All I could do was do the best I could.

As with any trial, there was something for me to learn. This condition further served to give me a heart. I felt deeply for the other students who had acne, because I knew what they were feeling. I still feel deeply for those who have this problem. Today, if you look closely, you can see I still have some scars. And there are some scars you can't see that I still deal with!

Can the gospel help you when you have problems with your appearance? It can. Personal appearance becomes very important in the teenage years. If mirrors could talk,

I'll bet they'd say that they see teenagers the most. Teenagers want answers to questions like, "How do I look to others? Do people think I'm good-looking? Do *I* think I'm good-looking? Does that special someone in Biology think I'm good-looking? Am I too skinny, chubby, tall, short, wide, narrow, etc., etc., etc.?" Unfortunately, the media has trained us to appreciate very few body types.

I'm sure you've heard the Old Testament story about Samuel the prophet waiting for the Lord to show him who would be the new king of Israel. When Samuel saw one of Jesse's sons, he was impressed by his appearance and thought he was the one to be king. Then the Lord told him, "Look not on his countenance, or on the height of his stature; because I have refused him: for the Lord seeth not as man seeth; for man looketh on the outward appearance, but the Lord looketh on the heart" (1 Samuel 16:7).

Sometimes what the world portrays as beautiful isn't even real. A few years ago, actress Michelle Pfeiffer was featured on the front cover of *Esquire* magazine. The caption under her photo read, "What Michelle Pfeiffer Needs . . . Is Absolutely Nothing." The truth is, she needed a little help to look that good. Brother Allen Litchfield reveals the rest of the story:

> But another magazine, *Harper's,* offered proof in their edition the following month that even the Beautiful People need a little help. *Harper's* had obtained the photo retoucher's bill for Pfeiffer's picture on the *Esquire* cover. The retouchers charged $1,525 to render the following services: "Clean up complexion, soften smile line, trim chin, soften line under earlobe, add hair, add forehead to create better line, and soften neck muscles." The editor of *Harper's* printed the story because we are, he said, "constantly faced with perfection in magazines;

> this is to remind the reader . . . there's a difference
> between real life and art."
>
> This is why you shouldn't be comparing your year-
> book or driver's license photographs with the magazine
> cover faces. The photographer who is shooting your
> picture is getting paid minimum wage, is bored, in a
> hurry, and may even hate you. Little wonder your pic-
> ture comes out looking awful. (*Sharing the Light* [Salt
> Lake City: Deseret Book, 1993], p. 107)

Some professional models have so much retouching
done, if you saw them in person you wouldn't even recognize them. In fact, supermodel Cindy Crawford is actually
a five-foot-two dockworker from Cleveland (just kidding).
When I was a teenager with acne, I would have loved to
have an artist to "clean up my complexion" each morning,
but I didn't. I just had to realize that under all that Clearasil
was a guy who was doing the best he could, and that God
knew who that guy really was.

While we're on the subject of appearance, let me ask you
a question: What if the quality of your life were fully
reflected in your appearance? What if any ugliness in your
life went right to your face? How would those rock stars
and movie stars, many of whom deliberately trample the
commandments under their feet, look then? How about
those who may not be very beautiful on the outside but
have lived righteously? Well, folks, as I understand it, this
is exactly what is going to happen. When we are resur-
rected, the quality of our lives will be fully reflected in our
appearance (see 1 Corinthians 15:39–42). Interesting
thought, huh!

My "Clearasil Years" also taught me another lesson.
There was a guy in my school who was very funny. He was
a senior at the time, and well liked by everyone. I remember noticing one day that he had worse acne than I did, but

it didn't seem to faze him. He was always happy and out-going. This really caused my wheels to turn. Perhaps those around me weren't as harsh as I had thought. Maybe I was overly self-conscious. Maybe my isolation was self-imposed. Maybe I could try out for things and do stuff in spite of how I looked! Perhaps if I could accept myself, others might accept me too.

If at First You Don't Succeed, You're Running About Average

In my tenth-grade quest to answer the question, "What can I be?" I signed up for the track team. I liked it. It was an individual sport, and it didn't attract the crowds like basketball and football, but I enjoyed being outside during the last period of the day, and I liked to run. I mean, when I first signed up I liked to run. It seemed as if the goal of the track coaches was to make you hate to run. I quickly developed a case of shinsplints, but I kept running. I ran each day until I was thoroughly spent. At the end of each workout I would go home and ask myself, "Why do I push myself to the brink of exhaustion every day? What is the point of all this?" But then I'd do it all again the next day.

One day I came home for lunch expecting to eat my usual pre-workout meal: a small piece of toast and a glass of orange juice. But my sister was home from school that day and, not knowing of my plans, had made me a huge bacon, lettuce, and tomato sandwich. Because I didn't want to make her feel bad, I ate it all. I went back to school feeling a little too full.

About an hour later, I was running laps. The coach had the whole team run in single file around the track at about 75 percent of sprint speed. The person who was at the front of the line had to run at a full sprint around the 440-yard track until he ran all the way around and caught up with the back of the line. Upon his arrival, he'd slow to 75 percent and yell "go," and the next person at the front of the line would take off at sprint speed. This continued until everyone in the line had a turn. Sounds fun, eh?

By the time I finished I was sick. Really sick. A walking time bomb waiting to explode. So I did something I had never done before: I asked the coach if I could leave the workout early. I went back to the locker room and took a shower. As I walked out of the locker room, finally it all came out. I won't use any gross slang; I'll just tell you I tossed that BLT all over an evergreen bush. Feeling a lot better, I went home and fell asleep. (I didn't tell my sister what had happened to the lunch she made me.) The next week I walked out that same door at school and noticed that the bush was dead. I had discovered a new herbicide: one BLT combined with a track workout.

Track workouts were hard, but track meets were really fun. In the spring I attended the state qualifying meet at Skyline High School. I remember warming up for the second heat of the 220. I was assigned lane two. One by one, the other runners came to the starting line. After the runners took their spots, the announcer gave the names of those in each lane. "In lane one," he began, "Mike Matheson, senior, East High School." I turned my head and stared right into the kneecap of the six-foot-eight, all-state basketball player. "Oh joy," I thought, as all five-feet-ten-inches of me settled into the blocks. "Lane two," said the announcer, "John . . . Bith, uh, Byth-way." He went on with the introductions; I positioned my feet in the starting blocks and waited. After some anxious anticipation, I heard the starting gun fire, and I exploded out of the blocks!

I had stayed after workouts and practiced my starts on more than one occasion—I was quick. I couldn't see anyone on either side of me at first; then the legs belonging to that six-foot-eight speed machine next to me began to

stride out, and I watched him pass me in lane one. I length-
ened my stride, I quickened my pace, and that day I ran the
fastest time I had ever run in the 220. But I didn't come in
first. And I didn't come in second, and I didn't come in
third, and I didn't come in fourth. I wasn't fifth or sixth, and
I wasn't seventh. I came in eighth. There were eight runners in that heat. As I crossed the finish line, put my hands
on my hips, and slowed to a walk, I heard a little voice in
the back of my head make a brilliant observation: "John,
maybe track isn't your thing."

But I also heard some other voices at that state qualifying meet. Although I had been soundly defeated, three of
the seniors on my track team spoke to me: "Nice job,
Bytheway." "Hey, nice try." "Good effort, Bytheway." They
had seen me at the workouts. They knew I had worked
hard. I suppose that, although I was still slower than
molasses, I had earned a little bit of respect for trying. What
I had learned back in eighth grade was still true: It is better
to be respected than it is to be popular. I had lost the race,
but I had won some respect.

Later in the year, I got my grade for track: C+. I was not a
happy camper. I shed some of my timidity and stormed into
the coach's office. "Coach," I said, "I've been to every workout, I've worked my tail off, I haven't been a slacker, and
the only workout I ever missed was because I was sick,
and I have the dead bush to prove it. I'm not the fastest
runner, but I have done everything you've asked, and I
think I deserve an 'A.'" Guess what? He changed my grade,
and I got an "A" in track.

Now, you may be wondering why I told you this story.
First of all, I thought it was funny—at least the part about
the BLT and the bush. But the main reason was to let you
know that we all struggle to find out what we can do and
what we can be. Don't get discouraged if you don't succeed

at everything you try! I didn't get a medal, and I didn't get to compete in the state finals, which means I didn't get a varsity letter. In fact, the only "lettering" I did in high school was in art class. But I'm really glad I ran track. I don't think that track competitions are very important to Heavenly Father, but I think that track competitors are. I learned how hard I could push myself, and I learned a little bit more about what I enjoyed, what I didn't enjoy, and what I wanted to be. Elder Marvin J. Ashton said, "True happiness is not made in getting something. True happiness is becoming something" (*Ensign,* November 1983, p. 61). Every experience, every setback, and every loss helps you to become a better person if you choose to handle it as a learning experience.

My Puma sprinting spikes would never again grace the track at Highland High (except during the Parley's Stake Family Olympics, in which I placed first in the 100-yard dash three years in a row: Neener neencr, Coach). So I decided to look somewhere else to answer the question, "What can I be?"

Sweet Sixteen!

Tenth grade is the year so many young people look forward to. Why? Because they turn sixteen! This means dating and driving! However, dating and driving demand dinero. Darn.

I turned sixteen in October of my sophomore year, and in December I was asked to the girls' choice Christmas dance. What a tremendous boost! A girl asked me to a dance! My date was a very nice girl from my English class. I barely passed the driver's test—after having failed it the first time I took it—and got my new driver's license the day before the dance. (Phew!) I was thrilled. My dad let me take the 1964 Dodge Polara. I'd show you a picture, but I don't think printers have that color of green. That car was known among my friends as the "green monster." It looked like it had showed up on the shore of a slimy lake with seaweed still clinging to the side. But hey, it was a car, and I got to drive.

We had a great time that evening. I mean, I did. Of course, I was a little inept with some of the social graces. I was still learning all the ins and outs of etiquette and manners. But I did know how to meet her parents, open her doors, and buy a corsage. She planned a dinner with some other couples at her house, and we went to the dance about 10:30 (fashionably late). I enjoyed my first girls' choice dance and I did my best to make my date feel comfortable. (That's not an easy thing to do in a car the color of Kermit the Frog.)

I don't want to say a whole lot about dating. I can't really give you a list of fun date ideas that would be any more interesting than what you're already doing. But I do want to remind you of a few things about standards.

The best summary of standards I've ever encountered is something you've probably already seen. It's in your little *For the Strength of Youth* pamphlet. I'm sure you have one, and it comes from a better source than me. There are only five paragraphs in the section on dating standards, but they make it very clear what the Lord expects. You've probably seen enough in your high school that would qualify you to write your own chapter on standards. You've probably seen people whose reputations were shattered because they weren't careful. You've probably seen others who will date only one person, and who severely limit their social contacts. Perhaps you've also noticed something I noticed in high school: It seemed like those who started dating and partying before everyone else got into more trouble sooner, and were more likely to end up blowing everything and getting a bad reputation.

I'll bet you have your own copy of *For the Strength of Youth*—and if you don't, you know where to get one. But in case you want to hear something about how you're gonna make it with respect to dating, I'll just say this: Young women, you will be much more respected for what you withhold than for what you give out. Don't date jerks. Date only those who respect your standards (see *For the Strength of Youth,* p. 7). You young men should be preparing for your mission and temple marriage, and improper dating is the most serious threat to your fulfilling those goals. In short, young men and women, don't be in such a hurry. Calm down and slow down! If you don't date much, big deal! You'll have your chance. Be young, have fun, and keep your standards high. Lecture over; you may be seated.

The Class I Would Never Miss

One day in my sophomore year, I was looking through the mail when a flyer from "Highland Community School" caught my eye. Apparently, night classes were being offered at the high school for anyone who wanted to attend. Most of the classes wouldn't interest the average sixteen-year-old, but one caught my eye: "Private Pilot Ground School." It only cost $18, so I signed up. Every Tuesday night, I went to class with a bunch of adults and learned about being a pilot. Flying airplanes had been a boyhood dream of mine since before I could even talk. I remember as a very small child being mesmerized by the planes passing overhead and wanting to fly one someday. Maybe that was what I could be: a pilot!

I tell you this because through that experience I learned something about learning. Think about it—at sixteen years old, I voluntarily took an extra class; I even paid for it! And I was never tardy, or absent, or tempted to skip out.

I hope that you can find something that you really love to learn about. I believe that the "three R's," reading, writing, and arithmetic, have been largely overcome in our generation by the "big R": the *Remote*. Television is a tool, but it can also become a weapon. If television is distracting you, delaying your homework, and turning you into a vegetable, then it's a weapon, and it's killing you. Television is a huge topic for another time, but I hope you will turn it off more often, and begin to explore all of the wonderful things the world has to offer. Find the areas of education that excite you, and develop a hunger and thirst for knowledge. Do I sound like your mom? Good. She's right.

The Fourth "R": Religion

I did a lot of physical growing during tenth grade, becoming the hulking specimen of manhood that I am now. I experienced some spiritual growth as well. One night I was in my room reading Section 19 of the Doctrine and Covenants. As I read, I felt something. I know you've heard stories like this before, and you may have asked, "How come this doesn't happen to me?" Well, I'd wondered the same thing. But on this occasion, it *did* happen to me. I felt a clarity in my mind and a peace in my heart. If I had to put what I felt into words, they would go something like this: "This is right, this is good, this is true." The feeling seemed to make everything clear. It seemed to increase my faith and let me know that all was well. To this day, I still remember very clearly that event. I felt the Spirit, and, more importantly, I knew it was the Spirit. As I continued in seminary, I seemed to look forward to my scripture study time, and I hungered to know more.

I also remember reading a Church book written for youth. As I read the following story, that same feeling returned:

> One well-remembered day several years ago, I stood knee deep in the Virgin River and looked up in awe at

the thousand foot rock cliffs of Zion's Park on either side. The park service brochure said that the rocks were more than 200 million years old. I remember comparing my age to the age of the rocks and feeling young, very young, very unimportant. It got dark early in the narrow canyon, and by late afternoon I could see stars in the narrow slice of sky above.

I recalled reading that scientists had discovered 7 x 10 to the 13th power stars. (The article went on to dramatize the magnitude of that number by saying that if there were 7 x 10 to the 13th power playing cards pressed together face to face, the line would go around the world six hundred times.) I thought to myself, I am one tiny speck, on one tiny world, that's going around one of those 7 x 10 to the 13th power stars. How small and totally insignificant I am.

That night as I unrolled my sleeping bag, a thought came to me with great impact: I am older than the rocks (for my spirit is eternal). I am more important than all 7 x 10 to the 13th power stars (because I am God's son, and they are only his handiwork). (From Paul H. Dunn and Richard M. Eyre, *Goals* [Salt Lake City: Bookcraft, 1976], p. 8)

When the pressures of school and popularity and fitting in would weigh me down, I'd escape into the scriptures and into some other Church books. They helped me to lift my perspective beyond my overpowering self-consciousness, my acne, and my snail-like 220-yard dashes.

These little spiritual experiences will happen to you, I believe, but you'll have to be in a place where they can happen. If you want to find out what the ocean is like, you don't move to North Dakota; you go to the ocean. If you want to find out what the Lord is like, you go where his Spirit is. And that Spirit can be with you even when you're all alone, reading the scriptures in your room. I highly recommend it.

Well, as tenth grade came to a close, I felt better about things. I spent a lot of time observing, and I learned a lot. I felt a little more comfortable with who I was and what I had to offer. And as time goes on, so will you. You're gonna make it, no doubt.

ELEVENTH GRADE

Fear, Risks, Tryouts, and Accomplishment

*God will judge you by the way you make
use of all your possibilities.*

Elder Marvin J. Ashton
Ensign, November 1983, p. 62

My junior year would bring changes to my life I could hardly believe. To anyone else, they would look like outward changes, but they actually began inside. You see, along with the acne, I had to get over another malady. It's called fear. I wanted to try out for things, to get involved, but I had a lot of fears.

Someone once said that FEAR is an acronym for "False Expectations Appearing Real." Each of us has lots of false expectations. Especially as teenagers, sometimes we think the whole world is watching us. We ask ourselves, "What will people think?" "What if I fail?" "What if I look like a fool?" And, for those of you buying prom dresses: "What if someone else is wearing what I'm wearing?" Sometimes we get so self-absorbed that it's almost a form of arrogance! As one wise writer put it, "You wouldn't worry so much what other people thought about you if you realized how little they did."

In my case, what finally happened was that I got sick and tired of being sick and tired, and I decided to change. These unsettled feelings had been building up inside of me for a long time—since December of tenth grade, actually, when I had attended the school's Christmas concert to watch my little sister perform. I also saw many of my friends perform, and it made my stomach hurt. "I should be up there," I thought. "I love music. I have *always* loved music." My cornet had rested silently in its case since the end of my freshman year, and I wasn't doing anything with music except listening to it.

And why wasn't I up there singing with my friends? Fear.

I guess I was too afraid to try out. My comfort zone had become a cage that severely limmited my growth and my experiences. I was so depressed that I left the concert early, went home, and buried my face in the couch. I did some thinking, shed a few tears, and made up my mind that I was going to get involved.

I knew I would have to take some risks, and I had a some choices to make. Should I run track again, or should I get involved in music? Both took place during seventh period, so I had to choose one or the other. Judging from my past performance in track, I decided to try out for Junior Choir. This meant I had to sing, by myself, in front of the teacher and many other people. But, I thought, what was the worst thing that could happen? I could get nervous, goof up, and not get in the choir. Big deal! If I didn't get into Junior Choir, I would run track again, maybe kill a few more bushes with my homemade herbicide. No biggie.

I have found this to be very therapeutic: When you're faced with something that makes you nervous, just ask yourself, "What's the worst that could happen?" Usually, the answer is not that bad. Sometimes false expectations make the consequences of failure seem bigger than they really are. If you and I are ever going to move forward, we've got to face the possibility of failure, and we've got to take some risks.

Risks

To laugh is—to risk appearing the fool.
To weep is—to risk appearing sentimental.
To reach out for another is—to risk involvement.
To expose your feelings is—to risk exposing your true self.
To place your ideas, your dreams, before the crowd is—to
    risk their loss.
To love is—to risk not being loved in return.
To live is—to risk dying.

To hope is—to risk despair.
To try is—to risk failure.
But risks must be taken, because the greatest hazard in life
is to risk nothing. The person who risks nothing, does
nothing, has nothing and is nothing. He may avoid
suffering and sorrow, but he simply cannot learn, feel,
change, grow, love—live. Chained by his certitudes, he is
a slave, he has forfeited freedom.
Only a person who risks is free. (From the "President's
Newsletter," Phi Beta Kappa, November 1982)

Everything we do involves risk. It's risky to get up in the morning. It's risky to walk across the street. Heck, these days, it's risky to breathe! Welcome to life! A ship is safe in the harbor, but that's not what ships are built for! Nothing ventured, nothing gained! Let's see, can I think up any other clichés? Aha, here's something better: Les Brown once said, "Life is like a game, and no one gets out alive: You can either die on the bleachers, or you can die on the field." I decided I was sick of watching the game from the stands; it was time for me to get out on the field.

No doubt you've seen the popular line of "No Fear" T-shirts. "No fear" could also mean "fearless," and "fearless" could also mean "full of faith" or "faithful." Having "no fear" is nice, but I like the other word better: "faithful."

I think that Nephi was one of the most fearless and faithful people who ever lived. Once he knew what the Lord wanted him to do, he would "just do it." Even though he failed in some attempts along the way, he would keep coming back, waiting for the Lord to "prepare a way" (1 Nephi 3:7), and He always came through.

Have you noticed, though, that even though the Lord was with Nephi, he didn't always succeed on the first try? It was on the third attempt that Nephi finally got the brass plates from Laban. Did he lose faith? No. He just kept coming back. And you should too. As you get out there on the playing field, I think you'll find that you learn a lot more from your failures than from your successes. Successes are easy to handle—but we always grow the most from the tough times.

Well, the time for my tryout came. I showed up in the music room at the appointed time with several other people. I sang "America the Beautiful" with no accompaniment, and I'm sure it wasn't that beautiful (my singing, that is), but, lo and behold, I made it into the choir. Trying out wasn't as hard or as horrible as I thought it would be. I enjoyed the class, I enjoyed the music, and I became friends with a lot of great people. And I felt pretty stupid for having worried about it so much.

One day, we were singing a song called "Up, Up and Away," and our teacher, "Mr. C," mentioned that it would be nice to have someone play the drums to accompany the song. After class, I asked Mr. C if I could play the drums. I had a really cheap drum set at home, and although I had never had drum lessons, I thought I could do it. He told me to bring my sticks and he'd give me a try.

All the next day I looked forward to Choir with a healthy dose of fear . . . I mean, uh, faith. Seventh period finally arrived, and we started to rehearse. Eventually, Mr. C asked me to come down and sit at the drum set. So I took my seat on the little drum stool and faced the whole choir. I didn't have any drum music; I just told Mr. C I knew the song and could do it.

As I adjusted my chair, I thought to myself, "This is your chance. Don't be nervous, or you'll mess up." I watched Mr. C for the tempo, "1–2–3–4," and we were under way. I laid into those drums with everything I had. My right hand was hitting eighth notes on the hi-hat, my left hand was striking the snare, and my right foot was pounding the bass drum. I felt like "Animal" on the *Muppet Show*—arms and legs flying everywhere and lots of noise. The drums were loud, and the choir was belting it out, and I thought it sounded great.

I was in my own world, crashing cymbals and wailing on drums, when suddenly I noticed that the choir had stopped. So I stopped. With the sound of the cymbals still ringing, I looked up at the choir, and everyone was smiling. Then I looked at Mr. C, and he was looking at me with an expression of surprise and a slight grin. The whole room was silent. Finally I said, "Was that okay?" He answered with a smile, "Oh yeah, it was fine, it was just too loud!" The whole class erupted with laughter. I blushed several shades of red; then I laughed too.

That night I wrote in my journal: *"Something I doubted would ever happen happened today. I found myself playing the drums while the Junior Choir sang 'Up, Up and Away.' I doubted that I would ever get a drum set, let alone that I would be accompanying a high school group."* Fortunately, a little faith and effort overcame those doubts. Later in the year the Junior Choir gave a public concert, and I got to accompany them on the drums (I played a little softer this time).

Fear? Not!

As I've read my scriptures, I've found that when angels appear to people, they often begin the conversation with these two words: "Fear not." Isn't that interesting? Heavenly Father doesn't want us to be afraid. On the very night of Jesus' worst suffering, he also told us not to fear. "Peace I leave with you, my peace I give unto you: not as the world giveth, give I unto you. Let not your heart be troubled, neither let it be afraid" (John 14:27). Speaking about that verse, Elder Jeffrey R. Holland said:

I submit to you that this may be one of the Savior's commandments that is, even in the hearts of otherwiᵕe faithful Latter-day Saints, almost universally disobeyed. . . . I am convinced that none of us can appreciate how deeply it wounds the loving heart of the Savior of the world when he finds that his people do not feel confident in his care or secure in his hands or trust in his commandments. ("Come Unto Me," Church Educational System Fireside, March 2, 1997, p. 3)

I hope you will always replace fear with faith. I hope that if you've been a little bit shy about getting involved, you'll take a deep breath, say a prayer, and take a risk. There are so many things you can do. It doesn't have to be playing the drums; you can get involved in silent ways, too. We'll talk more about this next chapter. Just remember, "no fear" means "full of faith"!

My Junior Choir experience was the beginning of much more involvement for me at school. Later in the year, I decided to take a bigger leap into the unknown and run for cheerleader. Yes, you read it right: *cheerleader.* I don't share this with a lot of people because they might think it means I was out there all alone with fourteen pom-pom girls. (Actually, that doesn't sound too bad.) At my school, it was okay to be a guy cheerleader. You had to run for this office, and the student body voted for you. Highland High School cheerleaders were more like the kind you see at college: They worked in couples, doing double stunts and gymnastics, and they also planned a lot of assemblies and other activities. It sounded like fun!

I worked very hard writing pep assembly skits, practicing back handsprings, and designing posters and banners. Finally, I wrote a cheer and performed it for the student body. After that, they all went to class and voted. I'll never forget later that night when the student body gathered in the school courtyard, and banners with the names of those who had won the election were unrolled out of the third-story windows. My name was the third to unroll. One of the things that affected me the most was not my newfound recognition and popularity, but the support of my loyal friends from my ward who had stood by me since seventh grade.

Personal Scripture

Well, I was going to have some huge responsibilities as a senior, and I felt like the time might be right to get some direction. I decided I wanted to get my patriarchal blessing. I think patriarchal blessings are an amazing thing. Have you ever thought what a privilege it is to receive one, to have the Lord spell out such personal direction? What other church or organization can offer such an incredible gift? President Thomas S. Monson said:

> The same Lord who provided a Liahona for Lehi provides for you and for me today a rare and valuable gift to give direction to our lives, to mark the hazards to our safety, and to chart the way, even safe passage— not to a promised land, but to our heavenly home. The gift to which I refer is known as your patriarchal blessing. Every worthy member of the Church is entitled to receive such a precious and priceless personal treasure. . . .
>
> A patriarchal blessing is a revelation to the recipient, even a white line down the middle of the road, to protect, inspire, and motivate activity and righteousness. A patriarchal blessing literally contains chapters from your book of eternal possibilities. (*Ensign*, November 1986, pp. 65–66)

Your patriarchal blessing may hold some of the best answers to the question "What can I be?" It can also contain cautions and promises, the fulfillment of which always depends on your personal faithfulness. President Ezra Taft Benson said, "I would encourage you . . . to receive a patriarchal blessing. Study it carefully and regard it as personal scripture to you—for that indeed is what it is" (*Ensign,* November 1986, p. 82). There's no set age for receiving your patriarchal blessing, so this is something you'll want to prayerfully review with your parents and your bishop.

There's another, more subtle message to consider in relation to getting your patriarchal blessing, and that is that your life is just beginning. If high school were the most important part of your life, someone would make sure you had your blessing long before school even started. There is life after high school, and your high school experience is not a forecast for your life. Sister Elaine Jack taught:

> What does a patriarchal blessing say? Have you ever heard of one which says, "I am sorry—you're a loser. Do the best you can on earth, and we'll see you in about seventy years." Of course not! And you never will, because of the divine qualities each of God's children has inherited. A patriarchal blessing is like a road map, a guide, directing you in your walk through life. It identifies your talents and the good things that can be yours. (*Ensign,* November 1989, p. 87)

I hope you will look forward to receiving your "personal scripture." The best is yet to come. Heavenly Father is just getting started with you, and you will yet have many opportunities to make a difference in the world!

Rebellion and Remotes

As a junior, I continued to enjoy seminary and learn more about the gospel. I looked forward each day to that time across the street in the seminary building. I loved it.

Unfortunately, not everyone attended, which I just didn't understand.

I loved the Church. It was—and is—very important to me. As a teenager, I never really went through a rebellious stage. Have you? I doubt it. If you're reading this book, I don't think you're the rebellious type. To be honest, I've never understood rebellion, especially against gospel standards. Rebellion is when you let others control what you do. That might sound strange, but hear me out.

Some people are under the illusion that rebellion means doing what you want. Some think it means being "independent." I don't think so. Elder Henry B. Eyring taught:

> When we reject the counsel which comes from God, we do not choose to be independent of outside influence. We choose another influence. We reject the protection of a perfectly loving, all-powerful, all-knowing Father in Heaven, whose whole purpose, as that of His Beloved Son, is to give us eternal life, to give us all that He has, and to bring us home again in families to the arms of His love. In rejecting His counsel, we choose the influence of another power, whose purpose is to make us miserable and whose motive is hatred. (*Ensign*, May 1997, p. 25)

Satan may try to get us to feel that we're not choosing his influence—we're simply trying to take control of what we want to do. Even then, someone else is really controlling us. To me, it's kind of like a broken remote control. Let's say you have a remote control, and no matter what button you push, it does the opposite. When you push "on," the TV goes off. When you push "volume down," the volume goes up, and so on. Now, here's the question: Who's in control? The remote still has control; the TV just does the opposite of what you ask! When people rebel, they may think they're doing what they want, but often they're just doing the opposite of what others want, so who's really in charge?

"I will do whatever makes people mad" is a different statement than "I will do what will help me be the best person I can be." Why in the world would I want to rebel against the very thing that would help me to become my best self? That's insane! I viewed seminary and the gospel as the way for me to reach my fullest potential. Why wouldn't I want to be there?

Because my parents recognized that I wanted to live the gospel, they were able to give me more and more freedom. By the time I was a senior, it seemed they had almost forgotten about my curfew. I guess I had earned their trust. Notice that I chose my words carefully: I said I *earned* their trust. It took a few years. Eventually they didn't even wait up for me at night, because they knew I'd be home when I said I would.

What Eleventh Grade Taught Me

Eleventh grade was fun. I took a few more risks, and most of them paid off. Perhaps the most important lesson I learned in eleventh grade is that "we accomplish in proportion to what we attempt." (I got that quote from a ski poster that hung on my wall.) It's a simple statement, but it's true. If you never take a shot, you'll never make a shot. And the more shots you take, the higher the probability that you'll eventually score. I had let fear, my "false expectations appearing real," cripple me for too long.

I hope you won't let fear cripple you. Fear doesn't come from God. "For God hath not given us the spirit of fear; but of power, and of love, and of a sound mind" (2 Timothy 1:7). There are so many things you can do, and so many things you can become. So keep trying! And your Father in Heaven will be right at your side. With him on your side, you're gonna make it!

I'll bet when you reach eleventh grade, you'll be more involved in your school activities. Maybe you'll even move closer to answering the question, "What can I be?" I hope so. Just make sure that amidst all the clubs and tryouts and activities and assemblies, your seminary classes never take a backseat. Out of any subject you study, the things you learn in seminary will have the most impact on your future happiness. Seminary will teach you about the most critical "tryout" of all, the one that lasts our whole lifetime, as described in the words of the Primary song, "So, little children, let's you and I *try to be like Him,* try, try, try" (*Children's Songbook,* p. 55; emphasis added).

TWELFTH GRADE

To Find Yourself, Get Lost!

The more we serve our fellowmen in appropriate ways, the more substance there is to our souls. We become more significant individuals as we serve others. We become more substantive as we serve others—indeed, it is easier to "find" ourselves because there is so much more of us to find!

President Spencer W. Kimball
Ensign, December 1974, p. 2

Well, folks, like the scriptures say, "it came to pass." Suddenly I was a senior. Life was a lot different from my seventh-grade days. I was taller, my voice was lower, and now I could drive and shave and everything. As the year began, it occurred to me that I had been reenthroned on the social ladder. Pam, the pretty blonde girl from my seventh-grade English class, was my cheerleading partner. And Steve, the student-body president I had dared to speak to in my eighth-grade science class, was student-body president again. But he was also my best friend. What a difference five years can make! Now *I* was the one who was in almost every assembly, so busy with activities that I was late for almost every class. Although I hate to say it, I guess I was also a little bit (gulp) "popular."

I had promised myself that if I ever got into that kind of situation, I would never turn my back on my friends or forget what it was like to feel alone. I'm afraid I got caught up in my "new life" at first, and I made some mistakes. But I think I soon got back on track, and it was really fun. I would try to give a lift to those I saw in the halls who were not in the popular crowd. In fact, I would try to say "hi" to everyone I could. If they made eye contact, I said "hi." Many didn't even respond, but that was okay. I remembered what it had felt like back in eighth grade when someone said "hi" to me, and I wanted to return the favor.

Of course, I still wasn't at the *very* top of the totem pole. No matter how far you go, there are always a few people you can never be cool enough for. It's always really fun to say "hi" to those people who would prefer to act like they don't know you. You know the type—they'll say "hi" to you if they're alone, but not when they're with their friends. High schools are full of 'em.

I used to love saying "hi" to people like that at school. Sometimes they might say "hi" back, but I could tell it really bothered them. The fact that they were too cool to acknowledge me made it even more fun. I'm sure I used to get on their nerves, and I have to admit I enjoyed every minute of it. I'd say "hi" to them every chance I got. Sometimes I'd just wanna grab them and say, "HEY, LIGHTEN UP! STOP ACTING LIKE YOU'RE SO COOL!" What's really interesting is to see these guys later when you get to college. Suddenly they act all nice, like you've been buds forever. I suppose it takes some people a little longer than others to realize that you don't have to act like an eighth grader forever. But I digress.

I'm not here to encourage the quest for popularity. I'd rather encourage you to be yourself and to live up to your beliefs. If popularity comes to you, I hope it comes because you are respected first. Popularity can be a dangerous thing. In fact, every time the word *popular* appears in the Book of Mormon, it's a negative thing. It can be a blessing to others if you use it right, and it can be a curse if you don't. I saw so much hurt associated with the boundaries that people draw in the name of "popularity" that I still have a hard time remembering my junior high and high school experience positively. Today, whenever I get a chance to talk to young people, I always tell them what I told you earlier: *It is better to be respected than it is to be popular. Popularity ends on yearbook day, but respect lasts forever.*

Be Your Best Self

It's really sad sometimes to see people who go to extremes to try to fit in. Some will act overly loud or

obnoxious, as if to convince others that they are not inse-
cure. Some will even act dumb! It seems some people will
do almost anything to be accepted.

There are others who don't quite understand the phrase
"be yourself." They take it as an excuse not to try to be better. Some get involved with extreme fashions, often with
the express purpose of annoying adults. (Hmmm, who's got
the remote there?) When asked why they do this, some
reply, "This is the way I am." Whenever I hear that, I want
to respond, "No, that's the way you've *chosen* to be. You
don't seem to know who you really are." The oft-repeated
verse in Ether doesn't say, "I give unto men weakness that
they may say 'This is just the way I am.'" Rather, the scripture invites us to come to Christ so that he can make weak
things strong (see Ether 12:27). The whole idea suggests
improvement! That's why I don't want to say, "Just be yourself." I'd rather say, "Be your best self" or "Be the best you
can be."

The fact is, when I was younger, I had no idea who I
was. I knew my name, but I didn't know myself very well. I
was continually trying to figure it all out. Fortunately, I had
the gospel to give me constant reminders. So do you. Each
Sunday at church, our identity is reinforced. We sing "I am
a child of God" and "I know my Father lives." The young
women stand each Sunday and declare who they are, what
they believe, and what their purpose is. Wow—if every
teenager knew the answers to those questions, no one
would be having an "identity crisis"!

Lost and Found

If you find yourself in a leadership position or in the popular circles, I hope you'll realize the power you have to
make good things happen. Through your example, you
have the ability to change your whole school for the better.
I hope you'll adopt the brand of popularity that shows

respect to others and makes everyone feel welcome. I hope you'll be a friend to the friendless, and offer smiles to those who have little to smile about. Later in life, you'll want to remember these high school years with gladness. Elder Jeffrey R. Holland told a heartrending story about a high school reunion. He was with a group of people who were gathering addresses and collecting RSVP's. He relates:

> In the midst of all that fun, I remember the terribly painful letter written by one very bright—but in her childhood, somewhat overweight and less than popular—young woman who wrote something like this, "Congratulations to all of us for having survived long enough to have a twenty-year class reunion. I hope everyone has a wonderful time. But don't reserve a place for me. I have, in fact, spent most of those twenty years trying to forget the painful moments of our school days together. Now that I am nearly over those feelings of loneliness and shattered self-esteem, I cannot bring myself to see all of the class and run the risk of remembering all of that again. Have a good time and forgive me. It is my problem, not yours. Maybe I can come at the thirty year mark" (which I am very happy to report she did). But she was wrong about one thing—it was our problem, and we knew it.
>
> . . . I cannot help but wonder what I might have done to watch out a little more for the ones not included, to make sure the gesture of a friendly word or a listening ear or a little low-cost casual talk and shared time might have reached far enough to include those hanging on the outer edge of the social circle, and in some cases barely hanging on at all. ("Come Unto Me," Church Educational System Fireside, March 2, 1997, p. 1)

You can probably increase the attendance at your twenty-year high school reunion by reaching out today to those who struggle. We're supposed to acknowledge the Lord's hand in all things, and it may just be that he put you in that position to see if you'd use it to serve others. In other words, your position shouldn't make you proud, it should help you to be humble. Consider this nice definition of humility: "Humble people don't think less of themselves, they just think of themselves less."

If you're not in a leadership position or the popular crowd, hey—don't even worry about it. Not for a second. Popularity, or even the quest for popularity, can be one of those spiritual eclipses we talked about earlier. Quietly go about the business of living the gospel, and try not to be distracted by the desires of the world.

Popular or not, your mission is the same. Your main focus should be to choose the right in whatever you do. Elder Boyd K. Packer said:

> It is the misapprehension of most people that if you are good, really good, at what you do, you will eventually be both widely known [popular] and well compensated. It is the understanding of almost everyone that success, to be complete, must include a generous portion of both fame and fortune as essential ingredients. The world seems to work on that premise. The premise is false! It is not true! The Lord taught otherwise. . . .
>
> Will we ever learn that the choice is not between fame and obscurity, nor is the choice between wealth and poverty. The choice is between good and evil, and that is a very different issue indeed. (*New Era,* August 1989, p. 4)

If popularity ever means abandoning your standards, it's definitely not what you want. Sister Ardeth Kapp said, "Never before in the history of the Church has there been such a need for young women who are willing to sacrifice popularity if necessary, suffer loneliness if required, even be rejected if needed, to defend the gospel of Jesus Christ" (*Ensign,* November 1988, p. 94).

Go Away versus Get Lost

A few chapters ago, I made a big deal out of the fact that Jesus never told anyone to "go away." And that's true. Jesus never said "go away," but he did tell us to *"get lost."* He said, "Whosoever will lose his life for my sake shall find it" (Matthew 16:25).

I think many of us have it all backwards. We want to find ourselves *first;* then we'll decide if we like serving or not. Jesus seems to be telling us that the way to find ourselves is to get lost in helping others. I'm not sure I would have fully comprehended that in seventh grade. (I'm not sure I comprehended *anything* in seventh grade.)

But perhaps you are ready for this kind of maturity. I do believe that one of the ways you can tell when you're really growing up is that you begin to focus on others more than on yourself. Throughout these pages, I've tried to tell you that you're gonna make it. And you are, but one of the ways you're gonna make it is by helping others to make it. Emerson once said, "It is one of the most beautiful compensations of this life than no man can sincerely try to help another without helping himself."

In an earlier chapter, we listed a bunch of things we could do to find out what our interests and talents are. Let's go through the alphabet again, shifting the focus this time to how we can help others. Ready? Here goes. We can: affirm, build, compliment, devote, encourage, fellowship, give, honor, influence, joke, kowtow, lend, motivate, notice, offer, praise, query, relate, serve, trust, unite, visit, wink, Xerox, yodel, and zucchini. (What's so funny? You could take your friends a Xerox copy of your favorite quotes, yodel them a song, and hand them a zucchini. It might sound strange, but that won't matter as long as the zucchini is ripe and the intention is sincere.)

One Last Plug for Seminary

I want you to know that in addition to graduating from high school, I also graduated from seminary. It was no easy task. By my senior year, I had become so busy that I had to take early-morning seminary. (I know, all you early-morning-ers out there are probably saying, "Oh, you poor guy.")

It's one thing to get lost, and it's quite another to lose everything. Remember, what Jesus said was that we should lose our lives *for his sake.* That means we always keep our focus on the gospel. If you get so involved in extracurricular activities that you think you have to cut seminary, you're too involved—you're out of focus! Instead of saying, "I'm so busy I can't afford to take seminary," you should say, "I'm so busy I can't afford *not* to take seminary." Seminary will provide you with the perspective you'll need as you get involved in all those other activities.

At the close of my senior year, I attended two graduation ceremonies: one at the high school and one at the church. I believe you will too. But before that time comes, I hope you'll do yourself a favor. Along with your scriptures, I want you to take a large jug to your seminary classes from now on.

> We come into these congregations [or seminary classes] and sometimes the speaker brings a jug of living water that has in it many gallons. And he pours it out on the congregation [or class], and all that the members of the church brought was a single cup. And that is all that they took away. Or maybe they had their hand over the cup and they didn't get anything to speak

of. (Bruce R. McConkie, "Seven Deadly Heresies," BYU
Devotional, June 3, 1980)

It's the saddest feeling in the world to approach a group
of youth with a jug of truth, only to notice that all they
brought was a little cup. And it's even more saddening
when you start to talk about some aspect of the truth, like
worthy music, or dating standards, or modest prom
dresses, and they put their hand over the cup and say, "Hey,
don't talk to me about my music!" "Don't tell me I can't
date 'til I'm sixteen!" "Don't tell me I can't wear off-the-
shoulder dresses!"

Please don't be like that. (I really don't think I need to tell
you that, 'cause not only are you reading a Church book,
you're almost finished!) Seminary teachers always love to
have students they know they can count on, students who
stand with the living prophet at all times. Be one of those,
okay?

School's Out

Graduation day came for me, just as it will come for you.
By the time you're a senior, you'll probably be looking forward to it. This book was written in hopes that you can
look back on your high school times with satisfaction,
knowing that you worked hard, you had wholesome fun,
and you made a difference.

Of course, part of the last day of school is the strange rit-
ual we call "Yearbook Day." You'll sit in your homeroom
class and wait for your brand-new yearbook to arrive. The
first thing you'll do is turn to the faculty section and reflect
with warm feelings on all the fine learning experiences
you've had with your teachers. Yeah, right. We all know
what you'll really do. You'll find your own picture first; then
you'll head out into the halls with your pen (this is the only
day of the year when everyone remembers one), and you'll

start signing. After several hours of composing such gems as "Please don't change," "English was a blast," and "I wish I would've gotten to know you better," you'll take your pen in your throbbing, writer's-cramped hand, and you'll head home. Then you'll find a comfortable spot and sit down to read all the messages people wrote to you. I'll never forget a bittersweet message someone left in my senior yearbook: "You're one Mormon I couldn't succeed in corrupting." I guess that meant he succeeded in corrupting some others. I hope not.

The interesting thing about that last day of school in your senior year is that, in large measure, the peer-pressure stage of your life will have come to an end. How will you do? Standing there in that senior cap and gown, will you be as morally clean as you were in seventh grade? I hope so. Will you be drug-free, alcohol-free, and tobacco-free? I hope so, because on this day popularity ends, but the respect others had for you for sticking to your standards and being a friend will remain in their memories forever.

Pomp and Sayonara

I was going to give the valedictorian's address, but I don't know where she lives (heh, heh). I hope you've enjoyed reading this! I'm sorry that so much of it was about my life. It's the only life I know about. To be honest, sharing so much personal information has made me a little uncomfortable. I just wanted to get across the idea that we all struggle through our high school years. I know I did, and you might too. But you're gonna make it.

The other thing I wanted to show is that the gospel was the most powerful tool I had to help me through all the ups and downs of junior high and high school. It gave me perspective. It gave me purpose. It gave me a reason to work hard. It gave me a reason to never give up. I don't know how I would have survived without it! Whether you find yourself in seventh grade or twelfth grade or somewhere in between, I'd like to encourage you to give your life to God. The list of rewards for that choice is outlined by President Ezra Taft Benson:

> Men and women who turn their lives over to God will discover that He can make a lot more out of their lives then they can. He will deepen their joys, expand their vision, quicken their minds, strengthen their muscles, lift their spirits, multiply their blessings, increase their opportunities, comfort their souls, raise up friends, and pour out peace. Whoever will lose his life in the service of God will find eternal life (see Matthew 10:39). (*Teachings of Ezra Taft Benson* [Salt Lake City: Bookcraft, 1988], p. 361)

So, how are you gonna make it through life? Simple. Give your life to God. Helen Keller, who had an amazing life despite being blind and deaf, wrote, "When you face the sun, the shadows always fall behind you." In your search for what you can do and be, avoid all the eclipses of life and face the Son, and the shadows of disappointment, discouragement, and loneliness will fall behind you too.

I wish I could guarantee that you'll never have another depressing day, but I can't. Life is hard, and you'll still hit some yucky spots now and then. In those moments, please don't give up! You're okay. Heavenly Father knows who you are, where you are, even *when* you are, and he has big plans for you. When you fail at the things you try out for, when you can't seem to figure out what you can be, when the person you're interested in isn't interested in you, when there seems to be no one around who knows how you feel, remember: You are not alone! Look to your mirrors: your true friends, your family, and the Lord. Remember what the Lord has said: "Let not your heart be troubled, neither let it be afraid" (John 14:27). Then stand up straight, swallow hard, and take a risk! Make a move! Go for a goal! You have a lot to give, and you can make a difference. The crisis will pass; it always does. So lighten up and enjoy the ride. Move forward with faith—with God on your side, you cannot fail.

There is life after high school. Your life is just getting started, and after graduation the fun really begins. Missions, marriage, and (brace yourself) more school!

THE END . . . or is it?

Afterwords

Hi! It's us again, a bunch of words! John's finished the last chapter, and he went to get a Slurpee. So, did you enjoy it? Did he put some good words in the right order? Was it more fun than reading the dictionary or a phone book? We hope so.

As we said in the beginning, words are really powerful, but in "the end" it all comes down to u. What are you going to do with what you've learned? Will it make a difference in what you've decided to b? I guess we'll have to c. One of the magical things about words is that they can get you to think. And then you can make decisions and decide to improve the way that you r. (G, this is getting old.)

Well, we've got to go. We hope you will see us again soon. We'll be found in lots of other good books, and we want to see you there, too. Y? Because you seem to be a very impressive teenager. And the word is—you're gonna make it.

Index